TACTICS OF WARFARE

Winning Life's Battles with Strategy, Discernment, and Spiritual Intelligence

By

Dr. Joke Solanke

Purpose and Pathway Publications

Atlanta, Georgia

This book is intended for educational, spiritual, and informational purposes only. It is not a substitute for professional counseling, medical advice, legal advice, or psychological treatment. Readers are encouraged to seek appropriate professional support when needed.

Published by
Purpose and Pathway Publications
Website: www.purposeandpathwaypublications.com
ISBN (Paperback): 978-1-968717-15-5
ISBN (eBook): 978-1-968717-16-2
Printed in the United States of America

Table of Contents

PREFACE

Growing up, my understanding of war was shaped by what I heard, not just what I saw. I vividly remember listening to the afternoon radio news as reports of blasts from distant nations filled the airwaves. To my young mind, war was national, communal, and always somewhere else. It was about bombs, borders, soldiers, and politics—never something that touched my day-to-day life.

But as I grew in faith and began to walk with God, I was introduced to a different kind of warfare—spiritual warfare. I encountered familiar passages like Ephesians 6:10–18, which spoke of the armor of God. I learned about the sword of the Spirit, the shield of faith, and the breastplate of righteousness. These concepts stirred something in me, but their depth was not yet fully real to me.

When I left the shelter and prayers of my mother's covering and stepped fully into adult responsibilities—career, leadership, ministry, parenting—it dawned on me that life itself is warfare. Not just moments of crisis, but the daily rhythm of existence. There is conflict woven into the fabric of life, often unseen and unspoken. Some people fight their whole lives and don't even realize they are at war. That is the most dangerous kind of battle: the one you do not know you are in.

Over time, I saw that warfare wasn't always spiritual in the traditional sense. Some battles are mental, emotional, or relational. Others are spiritual but masked in the physical. I've witnessed many lose battles not because they lacked strength, but because they used the wrong weapons. Some tried to fight spiritual battles with physical tools, while others misapplied spiritual language to what was clearly a matter of personal discipline, therapy, or wisdom.

There are battles you must not fight. There are fights that require retreat, recalibration, or silence—not engagement.

My decades of leadership in corporate America revealed yet another battlefield—warfare in systems, hierarchies, and human dynamics. This wasn't taught in Sunday school. It had to be lived, discerned, and survived. I've seen ambition dressed as loyalty, manipulation cloaked in mentorship, and envy parading as counsel. These too are war zones—just more subtle, more strategic, and often more dangerous.

This book is the product of lived experience, silent warfare, corporate betrayals, delayed answers, spiritual misdiagnoses, and divinely orchestrated realignments. It carries the weight of observation, the wisdom of Scripture, and the urgency of experience.

It began as a twelve-week teaching series titled *Tactics of Warfare on Divine Perspectives*, taught to equip believers not just to survive—but to fight from victory.

Now, it is a manual. A training ground. A war room in book form.

If you've ever asked: "Why do I keep facing the same battles?" "Is this fight even mine?" "What weapon do I use in this kind of situation?" "How do I win without losing myself?" …this book is for you.

This is not a book of hype. It is a call to arms—strategic arms. It will provoke you to think, to pause before you engage, to ask:

What is this battle? Where did it start? What weapon fits?

Because all of life is warfare—yes—but not all battles are yours to fight.

My prayer is that as you turn these pages, you will no longer fight blindly. You will fight strategically. You will fight wisely. And most of all—you will win.

Welcome to the battlefield. Welcome to clarity. Welcome to *Tactics of Warfare*.

—Dr. Joke Solanke

INTRODUCTION

"It Doesn't Look Like War"

He grew up in a hostile environment—but not the kind caused by war or crime. This was emotional hostility. A silent rejection he couldn't explain. None of the other children wanted to play with him. His presence irritated his own mother. She never explained why, but the name she gave him said it all: Sorrow. That name became a prophecy, a chain, a ceiling. It took him years to realize he wasn't just unloved—he was in a battle for identity. A warfare disguised as family.

Two brothers. One was carefree and the other careful. They were raised under the same roof, ate the same meals, wore the same hand-me-downs. But one day, the careful one succeeded—his offering was accepted. That moment of divine favor ignited a fire of envy in his brother's heart. He invited him for a walk in the field, perhaps to talk. There were no witnesses, no warning signs. Just a sudden argument…and a murder. A homicide born not from rage, but resentment.

He was a man of integrity, beloved by his community, and deeply rooted in his convictions. One day, after a dispute with a powerful couple, he received an elegant invitation: dinner in his honor. It seemed like a peace offering, a reconciliation gesture. But it wasn't. It was a carefully orchestrated trap to remove him and steal what was rightfully his. That dinner wasn't a reward—it was a death sentence.

She was simply being polite. A stranger had been in the neighborhood, offering kind words and warm smiles. He didn't seem dangerous. Over time, casual greetings became conversations. Then came curiosity, questions, suggestions...doubt. She let her guard down. He never raised a weapon—he just raised ideas. And with a few words, he severed her from her source. What she thought was a connection became corruption. What she thought was progress became eviction.

He was just trying to help. A family member needed support on a business deal, and without much thought, he signed on the dotted line. What followed was disaster. The deal wasn't blessed; it was cursed. And though he meant well, he stepped into a fight he was never supposed to enter.

He came to deliver food. That was all. But he overheard something—saw something—that stirred his spirit. He stepped in to help. Solved the problem. Saved the day. The people praised him…but his boss did not. What started as admiration quickly turned into aggression. The one he served became the one who sought his destruction.

He trusted him above all others. Gave him access. Promoted him to a position of honor and responsibility. He ate from the same plate, laughed at the same table, kissed the same cheek. And then…betrayed him for silver. Not because of hatred, but because of selfishness. The cost of that betrayal was not just organizational failure. It was death.

He was in love. Blinded by passion, he ignored every warning sign. She was beautiful, persuasive, persistent. But from day one, she was an agent—planted by his enemies to uncover his weakness. When she found it, she exploited it. He lost everything: his strength, his sight, his position, his honor.

He assumed that his role as heir was secure. But his inability to govern his appetite destroyed his credibility. When the time came to receive the blessing, his name was skipped. His indiscretion—buried in secrecy—had disqualified him.

He was quiet. Noble. Dedicated. But someone in the halls of power didn't like him. A law was passed—targeting his very existence. The justification sounded noble. But it was never about national interest. It was personal. One man's integrity was a threat to a corrupt system. So they tried to eliminate him legally.

And then there's the story that echoes through history: He was the people's hero—wise, powerful, and revered. But his closest ally, his most trusted friend, the one he never suspected—stabbed him in the back, literally and figuratively. Not because of policy. Not because of moral failure. But because of ambition, jealousy, and manipulation. The betrayal was so personal that when the knife struck, all he could say was: "Et tu, Brute?"

These are not fables. They are true accounts—biblical and historical. They don't look like warfare. But they are. Because warfare isn't always obvious. It doesn't always come with a sword. Sometimes it comes with a smile. Sometimes with silence. Sometimes with a signature.

The tragedy is not that people lose battles. The tragedy is that they never knew they were in one.

How to Read This Book

This is not a book to skim. It is a guide, a strategy manual, and a map through the terrain of life's many battles.

Each chapter is crafted with intentionality, grounded in Scripture, real-life patterns. To get the most out of it:

- Read prayerfully. Invite the Holy Spirit to highlight what's relevant to your life.
- Reflect deeply. Some chapters may expose past wounds or present battles—pause to process them.
- Journal insights. You will hear things in your spirit that are not written on the pages.
- Act on what you learn. Wisdom is not just for knowing but for doing.
- Share with others. This is not just for you. Pass it on.

May this journey awaken your senses, sharpen your discernment, and prepare your hands for battle.

PART I:

Fundamentals of Warfare

Chapter 1

Understanding Warfare and Tactics

Life Is Not a Game. It Is a Battlefield

You were born into a world that already had wars—some physical, others psychological, spiritual, emotional, or generational. To live is to engage, and to thrive is to win."

Life, in its most honest form, is not a scripted story or a peaceful garden—it is a battlefield. Not every battle involves bullets or bombs. Some involve words. Others involve silence. Some are hidden behind high-rise offices, under church pews, or buried beneath family names. But make no mistake—life itself is war.

What makes this warfare difficult to discern is how personal and unpredictable it can be. No two people fight the exact same battle. For some, war began in the womb—rejected before they ever took their first breath. For others, battle wears the face of a loved one, a system, or even a memory. You may call it challenge, opposition, trauma, or conflict—but I simply call it warfare with definition.

The Unchosen Starting Point

There are realities we don't get to choose—your birthplace, your family structure, your race, your economic class, your gender, even your genetic makeup. Yet these unchosen factors influence the kind of wars we fight:

- A child born during wartime faces conflict before understanding peace.
- An orphan battles rejection, identity wounds, and abandonment.
- A woman in a patriarchal culture may battle for education, voice, or relevance.
- A man in a broken home may battle emotional instability and lack of fatherhood models.
- A child born with chronic illness or disability may face battles others will never understand.

Even geography has a voice in your battles. Your zip code can determine your access to education, healthcare, and opportunity. Life is not fair—but wisdom doesn't waste energy resenting that truth. Wisdom prepares to engage it.

You don’t have to accept injustice, but you must understand how to fight it. Anger alone doesn't win battles—strategy does.

My Story: Fighting Loud, Winning Smart

I have lived this. I was an immigrant Black woman in leadership at Fortune 500 companies in the United States for over a decade. I call myself a triple minority—not just because I was Black, but because I was a woman, and an immigrant with an accent.

I was not naïve about the invisible wars waiting for me. I knew that when I stepped into the room, I was stepping into a system that would test my legitimacy. My performance could never be average. My competence had to be undeniable. I had to be so excellent they couldn’t ignore me. Promotions couldn't be denied, not because the system favored me—but because my results were too loud, too obvious.

But I watched others—brilliant, capable, well-meaning—lose battles they didn’t even realize they were in. They didn’t understand the power plays, the cultural codes, the unseen expectations. They brought average to a war zone and called it effort. In that space, ignorance wasn’t bliss—it was a setup for sabotage.

I remember listening to a woman born into a patriarchal culture that didn't believe in educating female children. Her voice was filled with bitterness. She blamed every missed opportunity in her life on her father. But then I met another woman, from that same culture, who—after leaving the covering of her parents—paid her way through school, carved a path for herself, and used her story to fuel her rise. Same battle, different outcome. Not because one was more spiritual—but because one understood she was in a war, and chose to fight with intelligence.

Whether we like it or not, economic, social, mental, relational, and spiritual warfare exists. Life demands readiness. To ignore this is to hand over victory to the wrong forces.

The Complexity of Battle

Life is also unpredictable. A friend today may be an enemy tomorrow. Saul once loved David—until David's victory outshined his own. A brother can betray another simply for sharing a dream. Joseph's life changed the moment he dared to vocalize his divine assignment. That was when the battle intensified.

Destiny is a trigger. You may not see it, but every step toward your calling attracts attention—both divine and demonic.

Sometimes the war isn't even external. David's desire to number Israel seemed logical—until you realize it was spiritually manipulated. Amnon's obsession with his stepsister wasn't just lust—it was a strategy from hell wearing the cloak of emotion.

Even success can be a battlefield. One careless moment can undo years of progress. A Goliath victory doesn't exempt you from a Bathsheba downfall. One unchecked battle can collapse every other.

Winning Requires Discernment

You do not have to fight every battle. But you must know which ones matter. A loss in the wrong area—like integrity, purpose, or identity—can sabotage your entire journey.

- You may win financially but lose relationally.
- You may thrive in ministry but collapse in mental health.
- You may be applauded in public but bleed in private.

Success in one arena does not guarantee security in another. You must learn to fight wisely, not just fervently.

Warfare is not always loud. It's not always obvious. Sometimes it is the quiet discouragement at 2 AM. The toxic boss who targets you for no reason. The shame that won't lift. The addiction that clings despite your best efforts. The betrayal you never saw coming. The inexplicable delay after you've done all that's right. These are not mere coincidences. They are battlegrounds.

Some battles you inherit. Some you walk into. Others are assigned to you because of your destiny. The worst are those you don't even know you're fighting.

Tactical Insight: Wisdom begins with awareness.

What Is Warfare? What Is Tactics?

"Warfare is not always visible, but it is always active. The unseen war is often more decisive than the one you can explain."

We've already established that life is not a game—it is a battlefield. But it is not enough to know that you're on a battlefield. You must understand the kind of war you are in, the weapons at your disposal, and the posture required to win. Otherwise, you may live unaware, respond incorrectly, or lose unnecessarily.

Let's begin by getting our definitions straight—not just from a dictionary, but from the trenches of lived reality.

Warfare Is More Than War

Warfare is not the same as war. War is the event. Warfare is the system. War may be short. Warfare can be continuous. War can be fought with guns. But warfare may never involve a weapon—just strategy, positioning, perception, and pressure.

Warfare is the sustained and often strategic effort to resist, oppose, sabotage, distract, or destroy the advancement of a person, group, or purpose. It doesn't always come with loud explosions. Sometimes it is slow, silent, psychological—and surgical.

It may look like:

- Mind games that drain your confidence
- Power plays that limit your access
- Systems that were built to exclude you
- Spiritual resistance that makes everything feel uphill
- Internal confusion that keeps you doubting yourself

Warfare shows up through manipulation, propaganda, control, sabotage, betrayal, and subtle opposition. And if you cannot see it, you cannot fight it.

The Many Faces of Warfare

Warfare is not just one thing. It has layers, intensities, and battlefronts. And depending on the season, you may be attacked in one, two, or all of them.

Type of Warfare | What It Looks Like

Spiritual | Unseen resistance to your calling, family, health, or peace. Mental | Confusion, self-doubt, anxiety, intellectual exhaustion. Emotional | Cycles of rejection, abandonment, or unhealed trauma. Relational | Toxic ties, betrayal, manipulation, or spiritual abuse. Systemic | Racism, sexism, injustice, exclusion, ageism, classism. Internal | The war within—between your habits and your healing, your potential and your procrastination.

Sometimes, the battle is not with demons. It's with systems. Sometimes, the problem is not your weakness. It's your unawareness. And until you recognize the form warfare is taking, you may waste precious energy fighting shadows while ignoring the real enemy.

What Then Are Tactics?

If warfare is the battle, tactics are the moves. Tactics are the intentional methods and strategies used to navigate, resist, and win in the face of conflict or opposition. They are your responses, your adjustments, your postures, your prayers, and your decisions.

"Warfare without tactics is like entering a battle without a shield or strategy."

Tactics are not just spiritual—they are practical. They are not just emotional—they are intelligent. They are not just theoretical—they are necessary.

Obedience as a Tactic: The Passover Night

When the Israelites were instructed to stay indoors and apply blood to their doorposts, they weren't told to raise swords. They were told to obey.

That night, obedience was a tactic of preservation. The battle wasn't theirs to fight, but their survival depended on following divine instruction.

Some wars are won by obedience. Some by silence. Some by separation. Some by showing up with undeniable results.

The key is to discern the battlefront and apply the right tactic.

The Danger of Mislabeling the War

If you think it's just life being hard, you'll pray casually. If you think it's just people being mean, you'll forgive carelessly. If you think it's just "your cross to bear," you'll stay too long in bondage.

That's how people lose battles that were winnable.

You cannot afford to be passive. You cannot afford to be average. You must become tactical in how you live, how you lead, how you speak, and how you move.

Some people are not failing because they are weak. They are failing because they are un-tactical.

Victory is never accidental. Whether spiritual, emotional, mental, or systemic—every battle requires a tailored approach. While the terrain may differ, certain principles are consistent:

- **Recognition** You cannot fight what you fail to discern. Every war has its own terrain, language, and players. Before you react, identify the nature of your battle. Is it spiritual resistance? Systemic injustice? A mindset war within yourself?
- **Repositioning** Sometimes, the shift needed is not in your enemy but in your posture. Discern the demand of the battle. Some wars require silence, others

require confrontation. Some require wisdom, not strength. Adjust your mindset accordingly.

- **Response** Precision is more powerful than panic. Winning doesn't always mean striking first. Timing, strategy, and restraint are often more effective than aggression. Let your response be guided—not by emotion, but by intelligence.

These principles will appear repeatedly throughout this book—not as theories, but as actionable truths to apply in your own battles. Some will challenge your instinct. Others will confirm your experience. All will prepare you to fight with strategy, discernment, and spiritual intelligence.

Transitioning Forward: Civilian vs. Military Mindset

Now that we've defined what warfare and tactics are, we must tackle the next critical element: mindset. Because you can't win spiritual, emotional, or systemic battles with a civilian mindset. You need to think, walk, and act like a soldier.

Let's explore what that means next.

Civilian vs. Military Mindset

In times of conflict, those without preparation suffer the most. This isn't just a metaphor—it is a historical fact. In nearly every major war—whether global or local, ancient or modern—civilians have consistently borne the greatest losses.

Why? Because they are not trained for war. They are not conditioned to expect it. Their survival systems are not built for it.

The Danger of a Civilian Mindset

A civilian mindset is shaped by assumptions of peace, fairness, and normalcy. It is wired for comfort, convenience, and control. It often expects that good intentions, talent, or favor will be enough to succeed in life.

But a military mindset understands that peace is not the default—it is the product of vigilance. This mindset is alert, strategic, and trained to act when opposition arises.

A civilian waits until war breaks out to prepare. A soldier trains before the first shot is fired.

Many people lose the battle of life not because they lack potential, but because they lacked preparation. They enter systems—jobs, relationships, ministries, even new seasons—assuming that what they carry will speak for itself. But life doesn't respond to assumptions; it responds to strategy and understanding.

Real-World Evidence: Civilian Casualties in War

In the Second World War, over 60% of the deaths were civilian. In modern conflict zones like Syria, Sudan, and Ukraine, civilians—especially women and children—are often the majority of casualties.

They didn't die because they were guilty. They died because they were unprepared.

Likewise, in the battles of life, you don't lose because you are weak or unworthy. You lose because you didn't realize the terrain had changed. You didn't sense the battle lines had been drawn.

You Can't Train During Battle

One of the greatest illusions is believing that you'll rise to the occasion when the time comes. But in warfare, you do not rise—you revert to your level of training.

You cannot build a fortress in the middle of an earthquake. You cannot learn combat after being surrounded. You cannot download discernment when deception has already taken root.

Training happens before the battle so that you can win during the battle.

It is not too late to train. But it is dangerous to wait.

Spiritual Insight: Soldiers, Not Civilians

Paul wrote to Timothy:

"You therefore must endure hardship as a good soldier of Jesus Christ." — 2 Timothy 2:3 (NKJV)

He didn't call him a civilian, spectator, or observer. He called him a soldier—someone equipped to face hardship, conditioned to endure pressure, and trained to engage with precision.

Long before the modern age of warfare, Charlotte Elliott captured the urgency and vigilance required of every believer in her 1839 hymn "Christian, Seek Not Yet Repose." She understood that warfare is not always visible—but it is always present. Her words are a call to alertness and readiness:

Christian, seek not yet repose,
Hear thy guardian angel say;
Thou art in the midst of foes:
Watch and pray.
Principalities and powers,
Mustering their unseen array,
Wait for thine unguarded hours:
Watch and pray.

This hymn is not poetic exaggeration—it is divine perspective.

You are not in neutral territory. You are in contested space.

Rest is not granted to the untrained. Rest is the fruit of victory.

Understanding Your Posture and Purpose in Battle

Your posture in battle determines your position. Your purpose in battle determines your strategy.

When warfare erupts in any area of life—whether spiritual, emotional, mental, relational, or systemic—how you show up matters. A soldier who crouches when they should charge will be overrun. A warrior who wields the wrong weapon will be ineffective.

Posture: Are You Standing, Hiding, or Advancing?

Posture speaks of your readiness, response, and resilience. In spiritual warfare, posture is not just physical—it is mental and spiritual.

Some show up to battle unaware, unarmed, and uncertain. Others show up fully dressed but mentally defeated. And yet others approach the battlefield alert, aligned, and anointed—ready to stand their ground or take new territory.

"Be strong in the Lord and in the power of His might. Put on the whole armor of God, that you may be able to stand against the wiles of the devil." — Ephesians 6:10–11 (NKJV)

The instruction was not to retreat or panic. It was to stand—in strength, in armor, in awareness.

Purpose: Why Are You Even in This Battle?

Not every battle is your assignment. Not every confrontation deserves your attention. But when God allows a battle—it's never random.

Some battles come to birth something in you— Endurance, wisdom, humility, spiritual authority, capacity, or inner strength.

Other battles come to break something off you— Pride, fear, disobedience, emotional dependencies, harmful habits, or limiting beliefs.

Still others come to build something through you— A testimony, a platform, a deliverance, a legacy, a movement, or a mantle.

Yet there are battles allowed to reveal what must be resisted. These are battles that come to steal, kill, and destroy—Peace, purpose, identity, relationships, vision, or resources.

You cannot treat every battle the same. You must discern:

- Is this battle a pruning?
- Is this battle an attack?
- Is this battle an opportunity for glory?

"Shall I pursue this troop? Shall I overtake them?" — 1 Samuel 30:8 (NKJV)

He didn't just react. He inquired. He sought divine instruction before engaging human pursuit.

Know the Terrain. Know the Target. Know Yourself.

Victory is not about fighting more; it's about fighting right.

- Know the terrain: Is this a spiritual attack, a soul wound, or a systemic oppression?
- Know the target: Is the enemy external, internal, or invisible?
- Know yourself: Are you walking in obedience, alignment, and spiritual authority?

You can't fight spiritual battles with carnal responses. And you can't win divine battles with emotional reactions.

Clarity of purpose in battle helps you conserve energy, avoid distraction, and secure strategic victory.

Reflection Recap: Tactical Awareness Begins with Clarity

Warfare is more than external conflict—it's a clash of systems, mindsets, spirits, and assignments. It shows up in everyday life. It hides in plain sight.

This chapter has helped you:

- Define warfare beyond the narrow view of traditional war.
- Recognize the terrains of battle: spiritual, emotional, mental, systemic, and internal.
- Understand that without preparation, even the most gifted can fall prey.
- Expose the dangers of a civilian mindset in a world that demands readiness.

You are not powerless, and you are not alone. But you must be alert. You must be strategic. You must be trained.

Tactical Activation: Engage with Intentionality

Before moving forward, take time to engage these 5 Tactical Reflection Prompts. Your responses will shape your posture for the rest of this book.

1. Where am I currently experiencing the most pressure or resistance? (Is it spiritual, mental, emotional, relational, economic, health-related, or systemic?)
2. Have I been approaching life like a civilian or a soldier? (Where have I lacked readiness or underestimated the terrain?)
3. What battle am I in that I've been ignoring, avoiding, or misdiagnosing? (Is it a test to build me, a war to fight, or a system to exit?)
4. What mindset or habit is sabotaging my response to battle? (Comfort, fear, pride, comparison, complacency?)
5. Where is God calling me to train, sharpen, or prepare now—before the next round begins? (Your delay in training could cost you more than you realize.)

Write your answers down. Pray over them. Use them as your tactical map.

Victory doesn't begin on the battlefield. It begins in your clarity.

Chapter 2

The Domains of Warfare

Different Terrains, Different Tactics

"Every battle is not the same. Every terrain demands a different tactic."

In natural warfare, armies are divided not just by function—but by terrain. The Navy, the Army, and the Air Force are all soldiers. But each one is trained for a different environment.

- The Army operates on land—boots on the ground, direct contact, strategic advancement.
- The Navy dominates the sea—maneuvering vast waters, anchoring territory, launching from below.

- The Air Force rules the skies—surveying from above, targeting with accuracy, operating in a higher dimension.

Each branch is necessary. But each one is effective only within its assigned domain.

A Navy officer dropped into enemy land without preparation is exposed. An Army soldier assigned to air combat without flight training is endangered. An Air Force pilot placed underwater without naval tools is ineffective.

Same uniform. Same mission. Different domain.

So it is with the battles of life. Just because you're familiar with one type of warfare doesn't mean you're ready for all. Some battles will meet you on the ground—in daily routines, relationships, finances, or your physical body. Others will come through the air—unseen thoughts, spiritual atmospheres, accusations, warfare in dreams, or demonic interference. Still others will come like tidal waves—slow, silent systems that seek to drown your purpose over time.

You can't use the same weapon in every battle. You can't win a sky battle with a ground tactic.

That is the error many believers make. They carry the mindset of infantry into the terrain of aerial warfare. Or they use land-based tools to fight an underwater current. And when the warfare persists, they assume something is wrong with them—rather than realizing they've entered a new domain that requires new strategy.

"Discerning the domain of your warfare is the first key to discerning your response."

This chapter will train you to identify where your battle is taking place—whether in the spirit, the soul, or the body—and how to respond accordingly. Because in the realm of warfare, ignorance is not innocence. It is exposure.

When I left the shelter and prayers of my mother's covering and stepped fully into adult responsibilities—career, leadership, ministry, parenting—it dawned on me that life itself is warfare. Not just moments of crisis, but the daily rhythm of existence. There is conflict woven into the fabric of life, often unseen and unspoken. Some people fight their whole lives and don't even realize they are at war. That is the most dangerous kind of battle: the one you do not know you are in. Over time, I saw that warfare wasn't always spiritual in the traditional sense. Some battles are mental, emotional, or relational. Others are spiritual but masked in the physical. I've witnessed many lose battles not because they lacked strength—but because they used the wrong weapons. Some tried to fight spiritual battles with physical tools, while others misapplied spiritual language to what was clearly a matter of personal discipline, therapy, or wisdom. There are battles you must not fight. There are fights that require retreat, recalibration, or silence—not engagement.

"Now may the God of peace Himself sanctify you completely; and may your whole spirit, soul, and body be preserved blameless at the coming of our Lord Jesus Christ." — 1 Thessalonians 5:23 (NKJV)

This is not symbolic language. Paul, under divine inspiration, names the three distinct dimensions that make up man. You are not your body. You are a spirit, you have a soul, and you live in a body.

Each realm plays a role in how battles are fought—and how they are won or lost.

When one realm is compromised, it eventually pulls the others down with it. A spiritually vibrant man can still live in emotional confusion or financial bondage. A physically healthy person can be spiritually blind. A soul rich in intellect may still yield to deception because the spirit is disengaged.

To fight wisely, you must first understand yourself.

1. The Spirit

Also called the inner man or the hidden man of the heart, your spirit is the access point between two invisible realms: the divine and the demonic. It is the part of you that engages in spiritual activity—whether prayer, discernment, revelation, or warfare.

This is where victory is secured—or lost—before anything manifests outwardly.

"But there is a spirit in man, and the breath of the Almighty gives him understanding." — Job 32:8 (NKJV)

True understanding doesn't come from intellect. It originates in the spirit.

You can be physically alive and spiritually dead. You can be gifted and still spiritually dull. You can even be a minister of the gospel and still be under spiritual oppression—because a disengaged or weakened spirit cannot discern warfare or resist evil.

Some are used by satanic forces unknowingly due to spiritual deadness. Others, knowingly, align with darkness. The spirit realm is neutral to access—only alignment determines outcome.

Your spiritual posture sets the tone for your victory. Without a strong spirit, discernment is lost, direction is blurred, and warfare is compromised.

2. The Soul

The soul is also invisible, but highly expressive. It houses your mind, will, emotions, intellect, and imagination. It processes what your spirit discerns and what your body experiences.

However, the soul is not a leader. It responds—either to the spirit or to the flesh.

"Why are you cast down, O my soul? And why are you disquieted within me?" — Psalm 42:11 (NKJV)

When Jesus said in Gethsemane, "My soul is sorrowful unto death," it was not a lack of spiritual clarity—it was a soul carrying the weight of destiny. The spirit knew what to do, but the soul carried the emotional burden of obedience.

Dreams received in the spirit can affect the soul. Delays experienced in the body can cast the soul down. Rejection, grief, betrayal, trauma—all are processed in the soul, and if unresolved, become open doors for mental, emotional, or even spiritual breakdown.

The soul's health depends on its source of nourishment: if the flesh feeds it, the soul becomes carnal. If the spirit feeds it, the soul aligns with purpose.

"The soul that sins shall die..." — Ezekiel 18:20 (NKJV)

This is not just about sin—it's about burden. The soul carries the consequences of what the spirit or the body allows.

The Body

The body is the most visible and the most attended to. It is the seat of execution—where consequences are felt, pain is experienced, and battles become real. It houses the soul and spirit, but it is not meant to lead. When the body becomes the leader, chaos follows.

"Those who are in the flesh cannot please God." — Romans 8:8 (NKJV)

The body is not neutral—it is rebellious by default. It has its own desires, its own appetites, and its own voice. Paul warned believers to "mortify the deeds of the body" (Romans 8:13) because if left unchecked, the body will dominate the soul and suppress the spirit.

The flesh wars against the spirit—not passively, but aggressively. It seeks control. It invites temptation. It makes decisions based on pleasure, appearance, and immediacy. David's fall with Bathsheba began with the eyes—a bodily sense that fed into the soul and then produced rebellion in the spirit.

"The flesh lusts against the Spirit..." — **Galatians 5:17**
It wants the seat. And when given control, it destroys destiny.

Because the body is tangible and seen, it gets the most attention. For the carnal soul—one ruled by the flesh—desires are centered around physical satisfaction, beauty, indulgence, and pride. Yet the body was not designed to lead—it was designed to **submit to the spirit** and obey divine instruction. If it does not, it becomes the easiest tool for the enemy.

The triune expression of man - spirit, soul, and body—are not just theological categories. They are **functional battle zones**. Every temptation, conflict, trial, or attack you face will touch one or more of these domains. If you misdiagnose the source, you will choose the wrong weapon. And when you choose the wrong weapon, even right battles produce casualties.

This framework will become a reference point throughout the rest of this book. Every chapter that follows will build on this foundation. We will return to it again and again—because **strategy begins with clarity**, and **clarity begins with correct categorization**.

Discern the realm. Diagnose the source. Then choose the weapon that fits the war.

The Realms of Warfare

Having established the tripartite nature of man—spirit, soul, and body—it becomes essential to understand how warfare unfolds across these domains. Just as the military has land, air, and sea operations, the battles of life also occur in unique but interrelated arenas. These realms of warfare are not random; they are structured, layered, and often entangled. This section is the heart of the chapter—because how you categorize a battle determines how you confront it.

Some battles begin in the spirit, others in the soul, and still others in the body. But regardless of where a battle originates, no realm remains unaffected. A spiritual attack can manifest in emotional instability. A soulish conflict can spill into the body through stress-induced illness. A physical affliction can wear down the soul and open doors in the spirit. Misdiagnosis leads to mismanagement—and mismanagement multiplies casualties.

Man as the Primary Agent in the Physical Realm

Here's the first rule of engagement: the main player in physical warfare is man. Nothing happens on earth—whether by divine orchestration or demonic manipulation—without the cooperation or participation of a human vessel.

This is a legal principle in the realm of the spirit: spirits require bodies to operate in the earth. That includes both divine expressions (e.g., God working through Moses,

Esther, Mary) and demonic agendas (e.g., Judas, Pharaoh, Herod). Human cooperation becomes the access point for spiritual realities to manifest.

This is why the physical realm is both dangerous and powerful—it is where authority is exercised, consequences are felt, and outcomes are sealed. The spirit may initiate, the soul may process, but it is the body that executes. If man refuses to participate, some battles cannot unfold. And if man ignorantly participates, destruction becomes inevitable.

The Spirit Realm — The Ongoing Conflict Beyond Sight

Whether you are spiritually active or not, the spirit realm is never asleep. This is a dimension of constant engagement—day and night, seen and unseen. The fact that you are unaware doesn't mean nothing is happening. The question is not if warfare exists, but how engaged your spirit man is in discerning it.

Your spirit is the gateway to the realm of the unseen—both divine and demonic. When your spirit is active, alive, and aligned, you are more sensitive to what's taking place around you. But when the spirit is dead or weak, you become vulnerable—either as a passive victim or a willing vessel for dark forces.

Even when the body is asleep, the spirit remains connected. People often dream of attacks, only to wake up with real symptoms: sickness, pain, fear, or sudden misfortune. This is not imagination—it is a spiritual transaction that has crossed into the physical realm.

The Spirit Realm — The Ongoing Conflict Beyond Sight (continued)

Example: Joshua the high priest was spiritually engaged and ready to serve, yet there was invisible resistance (Zechariah 3:1–3). Without discernment, such resistance would be misread as personal failure or closed doors.

The rules of engagement in the spirit realm are not casual—they are legal, layered, and precise. It takes more than zeal to engage—it takes alignment, authority, and clarity.

The Soul Realm — The Silent Battlefield of Thoughts, Emotions, and Will

The soul is the most complex of all three realms. It is not spiritual in nature, but neither is it fully physical. It serves as the bridge between the two, and its health is influenced by both. The soul is where the emotions feel, the mind processes, and the will decides. And because of this, it becomes a prime target for warfare.

This is the domain where mental health struggles, identity crises, emotional trauma, and inner conflicts reside. Some battles here are spiritual in origin—trauma passed through generational altars or spiritual covenants. Others are triggered by physical experiences—abuse, betrayal, delay, rejection, failure. The soul absorbs it all.

Jesus, aware by the Spirit of His impending suffering, declared: *"My soul is sorrowful unto death."* — Matthew 26:38 (NKJV)

Even though His spirit was aligned, His soul carried the weight of His assignment.

Paul emphasized that the weapons needed in this realm must be capable of pulling down strongholds, imaginations, and every high thing that exalts itself against the knowledge of God (2 Corinthians 10:4–5). This means that thoughts can become fortresses—whether for defeat or for defense.

What your soul feeds on—whether flesh or spirit—determines its strength. A soul ruled by the flesh becomes carnal and confused. A soul aligned with the spirit becomes a conduit of clarity and discernment. And because the soul expresses what it has consumed, it becomes both a victim and a vehicle of warfare.

The Physical Realm — Where Battles Become Tangible

In the physical realm, battles take on form. This is where warfare becomes visible, painful, and inescapably real. Whether it's a health crisis, financial loss, legal entanglement, job termination, relational conflict, or natural disaster, this domain is where the impact is felt. And because the outcomes are tangible, many assume the origin must be physical too. But that's the danger.

The truth is: not all physical battles begin in the physical realm. Some are the manifestation of spiritual activity—either divine testing, demonic sabotage, or consequences of human error. Others are the result of self-ignited battles, born out of disobedience, pride, or misalignment with divine instruction. Still others are triggered by human enemies, systemic injustice, or environmental forces. This is why the physical realm is the most deceptive—it looks obvious, but it's often entangled with roots far beneath the surface.

This is also the realm where many decisions are made in haste—because pain screams louder than discernment. When everything looks physical, we are tempted to fight with physical weapons. We medicate a spiritual affliction, argue with a soulish wound, or ignore divine resistance altogether.

What you see is not always what is at war. Not every fever is just a sickness. Not every delay is just bad luck.

Understanding the complexity of the physical realm—how it connects to both spiritual and soulish activity—will help us avoid misdiagnosed warfare and wasted energy.

Each Realm Requires Its Own Rules of Engagement

Before we examine real-life and biblical examples, it's important to underscore this truth: every realm of warfare requires different weapons and strategies. While the effects of battle often overlap—spilling across spirit, soul, and body—the origin of the warfare should determine the rules of engagement.

You do not cast out what needs to be crucified. You do not rebuke what needs to be repented of. You do not fast for what requires forgiveness or strategy.

Many lose battles not because the weapons of warfare are weak, but because they are misapplied. What works in the spiritual realm may not address the roots of a soulish battle. What is effective in the body may be powerless in the face of demonic resistance. Misdiagnosis always leads to misfire.

In some cases, warfare is triggered in all three realms concurrently. A spiritual attack may ignite emotional turmoil, which then results in physical illness or relational breakdown. That's why discernment is not optional—it's a weapon in itself.

Victory is not just about fighting hard. It's about fighting right. And to fight right, you must know where the battle began.

With that understanding, let's explore examples where warfare was misread, misdiagnosed, or fought from the wrong realm—and what we can learn from them.

Case Studies

Understanding the realms of warfare is not theoretical. Scripture gives us real lives—real people—who fought battles across multiple domains, often without realizing where the war truly began. These cases reveal a sobering truth: misdiagnosed warfare almost always produces unnecessary loss.

What follows are not isolated incidents. They are patterns—patterns that still repeat themselves today.

Job: A Spiritual Battle That Affected Everything

Job's life collapsed on every front—family, health, finances, reputation. From the outside, it looked like a complete moral or personal failure. His friends assumed the problem was sin, poor choices, or divine punishment. Their diagnosis was logical—but wrong.

What Job was facing was a spiritual confrontation that began outside the physical realm. A conversation took place in the unseen before anything manifested in his life. Decisions were made in the spirit realm that later showed up in the body—loss of children, disease, financial ruin, emotional grief.

Job did not cause the battle, yet he carried the consequences.

This is important: not every suffering is self-inflicted. Some battles are spiritual in origin but produce physical devastation. When such battles are misdiagnosed as moral failure, the response becomes condemnation instead of intercession.

Job's case teaches us that spiritual warfare can masquerade as personal failure, and unless discernment is applied, even well-meaning counsel can deepen the wound.

David – Overlapping Warfare Through Desire and Spiritual Influence

David's decision to conduct a census of Israel was not merely a leadership misstep—it was a complex interplay of spiritual influence and personal desire. The Bible makes it clear:

"Now Satan stood up against Israel, and moved David to number Israel." — 1 Chronicles 21:1 (NKJV)

What appeared to be a routine administrative act was actually a spiritually instigated one. But Satan did not operate in isolation. The seed of temptation found a foothold in David's own desire—perhaps a longing for control, pride, or misplaced security. The enemy capitalized on this, using an existing thought to inspire rebellion against divine order.

David's inner meditations became the gateway. His soul agreed with a suggestion from the spiritual realm, and that agreement triggered a national crisis. The plague that followed was not just spiritual—it devastated the physical realm, claiming 70,000 lives.

This event underscores a vital truth: our desires, if left unchecked, can become weapons against us. Paul's admonition to think on *"whatsoever things are true..."* (Philippians 4:8) is not poetic advice—it is strategic protection.

David eventually recognized this danger and prayed:

"Let the words of my mouth and the meditation of my heart be acceptable in Your sight, O LORD, my strength and my Redeemer." — Psalm 19:14 (NKJV)

When the soul entertains unfiltered thoughts and emotions, it becomes a portal for spiritual interference that manifests in tangible ways. Overlapping warfare often begins with internal compromise and ends with external consequences.

Jesus: The Soul under Pressure

In Gethsemane, Jesus revealed something profound:

"My spirit is willing, but the flesh is weak."

His spirit was healthy, aligned, and resolved. There was no rebellion. No confusion. But His soul was under immense pressure. He knew what was coming. His soul received the information from the spirit and processed what the body was about to endure.

The sorrow was not spiritual weakness—it was soulish anticipation.

This mirrors how the human mind works today. When the soul imagines pain, loss, or suffering, it reacts before the body experiences it. Anxiety, fear, and emotional exhaustion often occur before the event itself.

Jesus did not rebuke His soul. He submitted it. He prayed until alignment was restored.

This teaches us that soulish warfare does not mean spiritual failure. Sometimes it means you are aware. Sometimes it means you are carrying weight that must be processed in prayer, not suppressed or ignored.

Naboth: A Physical Battle with Deadly Consequences

Naboth's battle was entirely physical—land ownership, inheritance, and legal manipulation. He refused to give up his ancestral land. There was no spiritual ritual, no demonic manifestation, no prophetic warning recorded.

Yet he lost his life.

This case reminds us that human warfare is real. Systems, power, ambition, and manipulation can kill just as effectively as demonic attack. Naboth didn't lose because he was spiritually weak—he lost because he was caught in a human power struggle he did not know how to navigate.

Not every battle is spiritual in origin. Some are political. Some are legal. Some are systemic. And fighting such battles without wisdom can be fatal.

Samson: Appetite as a Battlefield

Samson's downfall was not an enemy army. It was appetite.

His physical indulgences slowly eroded his spiritual strength. What he fed his body weakened his soul and eventually disconnected him from his spiritual authority.

Samson teaches us that not all warfare is aggressive. Some wars are slow, seductive, and pleasurable. Appetite, when unchecked, becomes a weapon against destiny.

He did not lose his strength in one moment—it leaked out over time.

A Wisdom Principle to Remember

Right battle. Wrong weapon. Unnecessary casualties.

- Job's friends used moral judgment instead of spiritual discernment.
- David applied physical logic without spiritual inquiry.
- Naboth stood firm without strategic protection.
- Samson fought external enemies while losing the internal war.

Because the cost of fighting wisely is discipline—but the cost of fighting blindly is loss.

The Authority of the Believer: The Gatekeeper in Every Realm

Regardless of the origin of any battle—spiritual, soulish, or physical—man's passivity or activity becomes the driver of outcome. Whether through action, ignorance, permission, or resistance, humanity holds legal authority as the gatekeeper of the earth.

This is not merely a theological idea—it is a spiritual law.

"The heavens are the LORD's, but the earth He has given to the children of men." — Psalm 115:16 (NKJV)

Man as the Legal Gatekeeper

In every realm of warfare, nothing manifests without human cooperation. Even God, in executing divine agendas on earth, works through yielded vessels. Moses was a man, yet he confronted Pharaoh, split the sea, and led a nation—because he aligned with God's plan.

Likewise, the enemy cannot operate without permission or access. In the case of the demon-possessed man of Gadara (Mark 5), even the demons negotiated access—first through the man, then through the pigs. Their power was illegal without a vessel.

This reinforces a critical principle: Nothing moves in the spirit realm without legal access. That access is granted or denied by man's choices, alignment, and obedience. Whether God or Satan, the legal gate to earthly influence is you.

"Do you not know that to whom you present yourselves slaves to obey, you are that one's slaves...?" — Romans 6:16 (NKJV)

Key Insight

You may not be the source of the battle, but your response becomes the determining factor.

Chapter 3

Setting Priorities in Battle

Discernment—A Must-Have Weapon

"The discerning heart seeks knowledge, but the mouth of a fool feeds on folly." — Proverbs 15:14 (NIV)

The greatest victories are not always won by strength but by sight—the kind of sight that comes from discernment. In spiritual warfare, it is not enough to fight; one must know when to fight, what to fight, and how to fight. This is the power of discernment: it prevents misdirected warfare and wasted energy.

Discernment is more than intuition or intellect. It is the spiritual ability to perceive beyond appearances, to identify hidden patterns, divine timings, and true motivations. Without it, even the most well-intentioned believer can find themselves fighting the wrong battle—or worse, fighting on the wrong side.

Discernment: Not Optional, But Foundational

Many believers rush into action, forgetting that not all warfare is immediately visible. Some battles wear masks. Some distractions look like opportunities. Some attacks feel like blessings. Discernment helps you see the truth beneath the surface.

It is no coincidence that Solomon, the wisest king, did not ask for wealth, victory, or long life—he asked for a discerning heart. Why? Because discernment is the first weapon in the arsenal of spiritual intelligence. Without it, the rest of your weapons may be misapplied or rendered ineffective.

Discernment teaches you that what is allowed is not always aligned. It is the tool that governs your alignment with God's priorities, ensuring that you are not busy in battles that have no bearing on your destiny.

When Good Is the Enemy of God's Best

Some of the most difficult decisions in life are not between good and evil, but between good and God. Jesus did not heal every sick person He met. He didn't answer every accusation. He walked away from some crowds. Why? Because discernment governed His choices—not emotions, pressure, or public opinion.

Likewise, Nehemiah refused to descend from building the wall to negotiate with his enemies. David chose not to retaliate against Saul. These were not acts of cowardice but of clarity. When you understand God's assignment, you don't waste arrows on shadows.

Wisdom Highlight

Discernment is not just about avoiding evil—it's about recognizing divine timing, hidden motives, and heaven's priorities.

Discernment in Daily Engagements: Emails, Conversations, and Commitments

Discernment is not limited to pulpit ministry or spiritual warfare—it applies to the mundane and the moment-by-moment decisions of life. You don't have to answer every email. Not every invitation is from God. Every question does not deserve a response.

Even Jesus practiced selective engagement. He answered Pilate but ignored Herod. Why? Because He had already discerned Herod's nature. *"Go tell that fox… "* (Luke 13:32). Herod was cunning, dangerous, and opportunistic. Discernment of character was Jesus' first line of defense. The right diagnosis led to the right weapon—silence.

Discernment helps you preserve your voice for rooms that matter, and your energy for causes that count.

In business, discernment protects you from misaligned partnerships. In leadership, it helps you delegate with wisdom. In relationships, it shields you from manipulation disguised as friendship. In parenting, it reveals what your child is not saying. In ministry, it ensures you don't waste virtue on emotional black holes.

Discernment is your internal compass in a world of noise, urgency, and distraction. It helps you respond—not react. It teaches you to pause before you post, pray before you proceed, and assess before you align.

Discernment: The First Weapon of Warfare and Wisdom

Solomon asked for a discerning heart. Why? Because with discernment, you can recognize truth in a lie, light in the dark, and purpose in a storm.

Some battles are distractions. Others are destiny moments. Some questions are tests. Others are traps. Discernment helps you tell the difference—and that difference will define your future.

Discernment protects your emotional health. It informs your relationships. It determines how you steward time, energy, and focus. Whether you're making a business decision, raising children, preaching a sermon, or navigating spiritual warfare—discernment is your early-warning system and your strategic compass.

Not Every Battle Is Urgent

"A time to keep silence, and a time to speak; a time to love, and a time to hate; a time for war, and a time for peace." — Ecclesiastes 3:7–8 (NKJV)

One of the most overlooked skills in spiritual warfare is knowing what not to engage. Discernment does not only help you identify what to fight—it teaches you what to postpone, what to pause, and what to pass over altogether.

In every realm of life, the pressure to react is constant. Yet those who win consistently are not those who respond to everything, but those who respond to the right things.

In a world filled with competing priorities and spiritual noise, urgency is not always alignment. Some battles are real but not immediate. Some enemies are dangerous but not yet positioned. Understanding divine timing is as critical as recognizing divine warfare.

When Delay Is Strategy, Not Cowardice

"You don't have to fight every battle the moment it shows up. Some victories require timing, not tension."

In every sphere of life—leadership, relationships, business, or personal growth—discernment teaches you that not all battles must be fought now. Some situations look urgent, but they are only urgent to the unwise. Delay, when guided by discernment, is not cowardice—it's strategy.

Sometimes, the most strategic response is no response—yet. Timing is a weapon. And delay, when Spirit-led, is not procrastination; it's precision.

Joshua: Leadership Requires Timing Joshua was not just a warrior; he was a national leader whose decisions impacted an entire people. When he captured the five Amorite kings, he didn't rush into judgment. Instead, he rolled a large stone over the mouth of the cave and sealed them in (Joshua 10:18). He delayed dealing with them, not out of fear but to prioritize a greater battle. Joshua understood that finishing the war came before delivering the sentence. When the time was right, he brought the kings out and executed justice. Leadership requires knowing what to pause and when to act.

David: When Personal Crisis Demands Restraint *Not every provocation deserves an immediate answer. Some battles are lost not because of weakness, but because of premature engagement.*

David was not in a neutral season when Shimei cursed him. This was not a random insult on a good day. David was in crisis. He was fleeing Jerusalem after the rebellion of his own son, Absalom. His household was fractured. His authority was being challenged. His past failure with

Bathsheba had already set irreversible consequences in motion. He was grieving, exposed, and emotionally vulnerable, yet still responsible for a nation.

It was in that moment, when David was weakest, humiliated, and under pressure, that Shimei emerged, hurling accusations, curses, and stones. David had the power to eliminate him instantly. His men were ready to act.

But David chose restraint.

He understood that reacting in that moment would be driven by emotion, not clarity. He discerned that this confrontation was not the priority battle. His silence was not agreement; it was discipline. He absorbed the insult because he recognized that fighting on the home front while the kingdom was unstable would cost him more than it would gain.

Later, when the kingdom was restored and order reestablished, David did not forget Shimei. He addressed it strategically by delegating the matter to Solomon at the right time, under the right conditions, with the right authority.

That was not avoidance. That was delayed justice. That was leadership under pressure.

In modern terms, this is the wisdom of not responding to a provocative message while you are emotionally compromised, knowing that clarity, timing, and positioning matter more than immediacy. Some responses must wait until you are steady enough to respond without self-sabotage.

Jesus: Delay as a Divine Tactic Jesus constantly modeled restraint. When Herod, a man He called a fox, summoned Him, Jesus remained silent (Luke 23:9). But when Pilate questioned Him, Jesus answered (John 18:33–38). Why? Because discernment, not emotion, determined His response. Even when Lazarus died, Jesus waited two extra days before showing up (John 11:6). Delay wasn't neglect; it was divine alignment. He showed up when glory would be the outcome.

Just because a battle presents itself doesn't mean it's your turn to fight. This applies everywhere:

· Not every email deserves a reply. · Not every social media comment deserves a clapback. · Not every crisis is your responsibility to fix immediately. · Not every meeting or invite deserves your "yes."

Discernment helps you separate the important from the urgent. As the Eisenhower Matrix teaches, "What is important is seldom urgent, and what is urgent is seldom important." Misplaced urgency can waste time, resources, and emotional energy.

Like Joshua, delay the lesser battle until the greater is won. Like David, recognize distractions disguised as drama. Like Jesus, know when silence is the loudest weapon.

The Five-Fold Diagnostic Framework *"Shall I pursue this troop? Shall I overtake them?"* — David (1 Samuel 30:8)

Before launching a counterattack, even after personal loss, David paused to inquire of God. He understood that timing and target must be authorized, not assumed. He did not let the pain of Ziklag dictate the pace of his warfare. He waited for divine direction before unleashing physical action.

Discernment is not a luxury; it is a life-governing system. In spiritual and everyday battles, clarity must come before combat. Not every enemy deserves your sword. Not every fire requires your water. Victory without direction is still defeat if it pulls you off divine alignment.

Whether you're dealing with spiritual warfare, emotional conflict, career decisions, or relationship dynamics, this five-fold diagnostic framework will help you evaluate before you engage.

1. Pattern: Is it recurring? Is it generational? Some issues are not new—they're recycled. If the names change but the outcomes don't, you may be facing a pattern that requires healing or deliverance, not just strategy.

· Is this battle a repeat of what happened last year—or last generation? · Do you see family trends that now show up in your personal life? · Are you circling the same emotional or financial mountain despite change in scenery?

Discernment exposes cycles so you can break them, not normalize them.

2. Persistence: Why does it resist normal solutions? Sometimes the fight lingers not because you're lazy or prayerless, but because you've misdiagnosed the issue. Persistence without progress often signals a misapplied solution.

· Are you solving a spiritual issue with natural tools? · Are you treating trauma as a time management problem? · Are you addressing symptoms instead of roots?

Resistance is often revelation: something deeper is demanding your attention.

3. Prayer Resistance: When Intercession Doesn't Shift the Battle There are moments when even fervent, prolonged prayer seems ineffective. Not because prayer is powerless, but because prayer without instruction becomes noise. At such points, the issue is not the absence of faith but the absence of alignment.

Even Jesus, in Gethsemane, prayed with deep anguish. Yet the Father did not alter the outcome. The cup would not pass. The silence of heaven was not disinterest; it was confirmation that the will of God was fixed.

David fasted and prayed for his sick child. He lay prostrate, interceding with intensity. But the child still died (2 Samuel 12:16–19). When the outcome was sealed, David rose up, washed, and worshiped. He understood that prayer cannot override divine sovereignty.

Saul sought God through the Urim, through dreams, and through prophets—but there was no answer (1 Samuel 28:6). The heavens were shut not because God was deaf, but because Saul had already disregarded previous instructions. Prayer is not a substitute for obedience.

"What king, going to make war... does not sit down first and consider?" — Jesus (Luke 14:31)

Discernment demands strategy. Even kings must assess capacity, motives, and divine timing. Prayer that is detached from instruction becomes spiritual guesswork.

Prayer becomes resistant when:

· You are praying about a situation but not praying from divine instruction. · You are engaging in spiritual warfare when obedience is the missing key. · You are rebuking devils when the issue is a decision, boundary, or correction God has already highlighted. · You are applying pressure in prayer where God is calling for surrender.

Some battles persist because prayer is being used to avoid responsibility. Others linger because repetition is used where revelation is required.

Prayer is most powerful when it is informed. Intercession is effective when it is authorized. Revelation fuels results. Accuracy shortens warfare.

4. Emotional Triggers: Are wounds distorting perception? You may not be under attack—you may be under the influence of an old wound. Emotional triggers can hijack reality, creating enemies where there are none and turning feedback into offense.

· Are you reacting more to your history than the current situation? · Does disagreement feel like rejection? · Are you fighting people who are merely touching a nerve, not throwing a punch?

Until you heal, you'll always misread your battlefield.

5. Spiritual Signals: What dreams, warnings, or divine interruptions are occurring? The Spirit speaks in whispers before He shouts. Pay attention to divine red flags—restlessness, repeated dreams, supernatural delays, or sudden clarity.

· Has a door you pushed hard on suddenly closed? · Do your dreams confirm or confront your plans? · Are interruptions pointing you toward something you've been avoiding?

Spiritual signals are heaven's diagnostics. Don't miss them because they're quiet.

Discernment is rooted in diagnosis. You can't win what you don't first understand. Examine the source before choosing a sword.

Discernment vs. Reaction: The War Within Discernment listens; reaction yells. Discernment pauses; reaction pounces. Discernment inquires of God; reaction assumes responsibility.

Many believers misinterpret emotional urgency as spiritual instruction. In the heat of betrayal, disappointment, or frustration, warfare seems justified—but if the origin is flesh, the outcome will not carry divine endorsement.

David's response to Shimei (2 Samuel 16:5–12) is a masterclass in restraint. Though cursed and humiliated publicly, he chose silence over retaliation. His discernment overruled the urge to defend himself.

"Let him alone, and let him curse; for so the Lord has ordered him... It may be that the Lord will look on my affliction, and... repay me with good." — David (2 Samuel 16:11–12)

David understood: not every insult is an invitation to react. Some are divine filters, designed to test whether your identity is secured in God or still dependent on vindication.

Discernment is divine intelligence. It knows when to act, when to wait, and when to let God respond on your behalf.

· Are you reacting to people or responding to patterns? · Are you driven by urgency—or guided by strategy? · Are you trying to prove a point—or pursue God's purpose?

Emotional impulse will always mimic urgency. But urgency without clarity leads to unnecessary warfare—and exhaustion without results.

Delays Are Not Always Demonic Even divine delays can feel like opposition. But some pauses are heaven's protection—not hell's interference.

"Jesus loved Martha... Yet when He heard that Lazarus was sick, He stayed two more days." — John 11:5–6 (paraphrased)

Jesus delayed—not because He lacked compassion, but because the timing of glory had not yet aligned. Had He responded emotionally, the resurrection testimony would've been reduced to mere healing.

Discernment is a powerful weapon, but it is also one of the most misunderstood. While it can reveal hidden battles and unlock divine strategy, many believers unknowingly confuse it with suspicion, fear, or gut instinct. Before you can wield discernment with precision, you must know what it is—and what it is not. Let's now expose the counterfeits and clarify the true nature of discernment.

When It's Not Discernment *"Every good and perfect gift is from above..."* — James 1:17 (.)

Discernment is a divine tool, but not everything that feels sharp or insightful is from God. In an age of heightened emotions and hyper-analysis, many believers confuse discernment with suspicion, intuition, gut feelings, or even fear-based judgments. But unlike these natural or emotional responses, true discernment is precise, Spirit-led, and rooted in truth.

"He does not judge by what His eyes see, nor make decisions based on what His ears hear." — Isaiah 11:3 (paraphrased)

Before we go further into how to develop this essential weapon, let us first unmask the common counterfeits of discernment.

1. Suspicion: The Offspring of Wounded Trust Suspicion often masquerades as discernment but flows from past hurt, fear of betrayal, or unhealed trauma. It draws conclusions without evidence, assumes the worst, and weaponizes observation without compassion. Suspicion watches to catch; discernment watches to protect.

2. Intuition: The Gift of the Senses, Not the Spirit Intuition is a natural faculty—an internal alert system developed by life experience, pattern recognition, and emotional intelligence. It is not evil, but it is limited to human perspective. Discernment is superior because it sees what the eyes and logic cannot.

3. Gut Feeling: A Reaction, Not a Revelation That uneasy feeling in your stomach may feel spiritual, but gut feelings are often biological responses to fear, stress, or previous trauma. Discernment is not felt in the stomach; it is received in the spirit. Gut feelings react; discernment reveals truth.

4. Witch-Hunting: Judgment in the Name of Revelation When discernment is reduced to accusations and finger-pointing, it becomes spiritual abuse. Witch-hunting uses "discernment" as a mask for control, criticism, and paranoia—especially in leadership circles. Discernment identifies fruit, not faults. It builds, not breaks.

5. Overanalysis: When the Mind Tries to Replace the Spirit Analyzing behavior, tone, or patterns too deeply can lead to false discernment. This is logic trying to do the work of the Spirit. True discernment is light, not suspicion wrapped in spreadsheets and overthought conclusions. Discernment begins where analysis ends.

6. Projection: Reading Others Through Your Own Lens Sometimes what we call "discernment" is simply our own issue mirrored onto someone else. Insecurity, jealousy, fear, or offense may cause us to misread pure hearts through a contaminated lens. Discernment requires a clean heart to see clearly.

Discernment is not a personality trait. It's not a talent. It is a spiritual faculty—a knowing that bypasses logic, dreams, and even visible confirmation. It is not sourced in fear, suspicion, or intellect. It flows from alignment with the Spirit of God.

"But there is a spirit in man, and the breath of the Almighty gives him understanding." — Job 32:8 (.)

You don't get discernment by being older. You grow in it by being more spiritually trained, more yielded, and more internally aligned.

Just as a pianist develops sensitivity to sound through consistent practice, the human spirit becomes trained in discernment by constant exposure to God's presence, voice, and truth.

"But solid food is for the mature, who by constant use have trained themselves to distinguish good from evil." — Hebrews 5:14 (NIV)

This means discernment is trainable. You sharpen it when:

- You obey even the quietest promptings of the Spirit
- You stay in environments that value truth over popularity
- You confront your own motives before analyzing others

- You saturate your inner man with the Word, not just devotionals
- You submit your senses to the Spirit, not your soul

Discernment is not about seeing demons. It's about seeing clearly. It is precision powered by purity.

Discernment is not spiritual noise; it is spiritual clarity. It is born from alignment, matured by obedience, and made sharp by exposure to God's truth.

Discernment in Action—From Insight to Impact *"Solid food is for the mature, who because of practice have their senses trained to discern good and evil."* — Hebrews 5:14 (NASB)

Discernment is not a mystical gift reserved for a select few; it is a vital weapon for every believer engaged in spiritual warfare. While it is fueled by the Spirit, discernment sharpens with use. What begins as a prompting matures into clarity through yieldedness and training.

Discernment in Action: Biblical Case Studies Discernment is not a performance; it's a perception. It does not always come through dreams, visions, or prophecies. True discernment flows from a spirit aligned with God, trained to know what cannot be seen, heard, or deduced naturally.

Throughout Scripture, discernment was the key that unlocked hidden realities and protected divine agendas. It didn't always come through thunder or angelic visitations, but through the inner knowing of a spirit attuned to God.

Paul and the Slave Girl (Acts 16:16–18) "These men are servants of the Most High God, who proclaim to us the way of salvation!"

Her words were accurate. Her tone may have seemed reverent. But Paul, grieved in his spirit, discerned the truth behind the flattery. She was operating under a spirit of divination, not the Spirit of God. After many days, he cast it out—not in reaction, but in precision.

Discernment reveals what flattery hides.

This was not intuition. It was not suspicion. It was not a pattern of behavior. Paul's spirit picked up what her lips tried to conceal.

Peter with Ananias & Sapphira (Acts 5:1–11) Peter didn't get a vision, dream, or word from another apostle. He perceived their lie in real time. His rebuke was swift, not because he saw the bank slip, but because he saw into the posture of their hearts.

Discernment protects spiritual atmospheres.

When the atmosphere of purity is polluted by hypocrisy, discernment acts as a firewall. Peter's spiritual intelligence preserved the integrity of the early church.

Elisha and Gehazi (2 Kings 5:20–27) When Elisha asked, *"Went not mine heart with thee?"*, he revealed a deeper truth: his inner man tracked Gehazi's actions without leaving his room. This was not a prophecy. It was not a vision. It was a knowing—a manifestation of alignment between Elisha's spirit and God's.

The Hebrew phrase is לִבִּי הָלַךְ (libbi halakh):

·

Libbi (לִבִּי) = my heart, referring to the inner man, will, spiritual center. · Halakh (הָלַךְ) = went, meaning to walk or travel.

Literal meaning: *"Did not my inner being journey with you?"*

This was not: · A vision (chazon) · A dream (chalom) · A prophetic word (naba') · Nor did Elisha say, "The Lord told me…"

This was: · Spiritual alignment and inner awareness. · A deep knowing of the spirit—not bound by time or physical location.

Discernment is not suspicion; it is precise, alignment-based intelligence rooted in spiritual proximity.

This was not surveillance; it was spiritual sensitivity. Elisha's heart followed where his feet did not go.

Key Takeaways

1. Discernment is Spirit-given—not self-generated.
2. It does not need to be dramatic to be divine.
3. It bypasses the five senses and relies on alignment.
4. It is not based on deduction, emotion, or instinct.
5. It safeguards the move of God by seeing beyond the surface.

"There is a spirit in man, and the breath of the Almighty gives him understanding." – Job 32:8 (.)

Part II

Special Weapons and Strategy

Chapter 4

Giving is a Weapon of War

"For God so loved the world that He gave…" – John 3:16 (KJV)

There's a tool in every home that teaches a profound spiritual truth: the kitchen knife.

In the hands of a skilled cook, it slices, prepares, and makes room for nourishment. But that same tool, when necessary, can serve as a weapon of defense. Its power isn't in its shape, but in its purpose. What makes it powerful is not what it is, but how it is used.

Giving is just like that.

To some, it's a routine. To others, a financial principle. But to the spiritually discerning, giving is a weapon—an instrument of victory when wielded with understanding, obedience, and revelation.

Many give as a transaction, expecting an immediate return. But in the spiritual realm, giving, especially sacrificial giving, is not about trade. It is about warfare, alignment, and exchange.

It can:

- Break through demonic resistance
- Birth solutions where logic has failed
- Silence accusations in the court of heaven
- Trigger divine remembrance and rescue
- Unlock covenant elevation

Giving predates Moses. It is older than religion. It is both a universal law and a spiritual principle, embedded in the foundation of divine operations. It is one of the most potent arsenals in the hands of the wise.

The battle for humanity's soul was not won by prayer or prophecy. It was sealed by a gift—sacrificial gift: "…He gave."

At the core of salvation is a spiritual exchange. The cross was a transaction. The resurrection was the receipt.

Giving is more than generosity. It is more than money. It is the mystery of divine strategy—a weapon for those who know how to engage it in warfare, breakthrough, and covenant alignment.

"While the earth remaineth, seedtime and harvest... shall not cease." — Genesis 8:22 (KJV)

"But this I say, He which soweth sparingly shall reap also sparingly; and he which soweth bountifully shall reap also bountifully." — 2 Corinthians 9:6 (KJV)

The Mystery of the Seed — Giving as Divine Technology

In the economy of the Spirit, a seed is never just a material object. It is a spiritual code, an encoded transaction point between the natural and the divine. The seed, whether financial, material, or intangible, carries within it the mystery of multiplication, exchange, and divine intervention. It is not merely generosity; it is technology. And like all technologies, its outcome is determined not merely by intention, but by alignment and application.

To sow a seed is to make a bold declaration: “I recognize this altar, this need, this moment—and I engage it by revelation.” A seed is a response to instruction, not an act of compulsion. It is not charity. It is not manipulation. It is a faith-triggered act of obedience.

The Logic of Seedtime and Harvest Genesis 8:22 introduces an eternal law: “Seedtime and harvest… shall not cease.” Though agricultural in language, this is more than a farming principle; it is a spiritual law of exchange. It means the outcomes of life, both spiritual and natural, can be regulated by what you release as seed.

In spiritual warfare, your seed can:

- Go where your voice cannot reach.
- Do what your strength cannot accomplish.
- Speak in courts where your history has no standing.
- Interrupt patterns that fasting alone has not broken.

When you sow into revelation, you authorize heaven to respond to the unseen.

The Widow of Zarephath: A Case Study (1 Kings 17:8–16)

In the heat of drought and despair, the prophet Elijah meets a widow preparing her last meal before death. The instruction comes: "Make me a little cake first."

Her obedience activated a principle that changed the trajectory of her family line. Her seed did not merely produce food; it suspended death, preserved her child, and sustained supernatural supply during famine.

Her miracle was not triggered by prayer or prophecy alone; it was triggered by giving.

Her flour and oil did not multiply until they left her hand. Breakthrough did not come with provision; it came through obedience.

Giving Is Not Always Monetary While financial giving is the most referenced form, the principle of the seed is broader and richer. Seeds can include:

- Time – when sown in service or consecration
- Honor – when sown toward spiritual authority
- Intercession – as sacrificial prayer for others
- Acts of Kindness – especially to the forgotten or overlooked

Each of these can open doors, provoke heaven, and shift spiritual atmospheres when offered with discernment and revelation.

Giving as a Divine Response The seed is God's answer to cycles. The seed is how you sow into a different outcome. The seed is how you exit survival mode and authorize increase.

In the kingdom, the seed:

- Initiates divine memory (Acts 10:4)
- Engages prophetic fulfillment (Genesis 22)
- Unlocks generational shift (Genesis 25:29–34)

Your seed leaves your hand, but it does not leave your life; it enters your future and waits for you at the point of need.

Giving, when aligned with revelation and obedience, is more than charity; it is a spiritual act of war. It can shift the trajectory of your life, override embargoes, and provoke divine remembrance. When the seed is released by faith, it becomes a spiritual code—summoning heaven's intervention in ways your voice or strength cannot. Whether through time, honor, or resources, giving as divine technology is how you legislate victory in unseen battles.

The Dual Role of Giving Giving is both a defensive and an offensive weapon for victory. Defensively, giving establishes spiritual covering and alignment, preserving what has been entrusted to you and limiting the enemy's access to your life, resources, and destiny. It builds a hedge against lack, fear, and instability by anchoring the heart in trust rather than possession, ensuring that what threatens others does not consume you.

Offensively, giving becomes a strategic act that initiates movement where resistance exists and progress has stalled. It is not a reaction to circumstances but a deliberate transaction that engages divine principles, provokes intervention, and shifts atmospheres beyond human reach. Through giving, what is released from the hand creates access to what only God can release, making it one of the few tools in warfare that both protects what you have and produces what you need.

The Altar of Exchange – Sacrifice and Spiritual Transactions *"And the angel of the Lord called unto Abraham out of heaven the second time, and said, By myself have I sworn, saith the Lord, for because thou hast done this thing... in blessing I will bless thee."* — Genesis 22:15–17 (KJV)

Not all giving is equal. There is a realm of giving that is so costly, so strategic, and so divinely timed that it provokes irreversible spiritual outcomes. This is the realm of the altar of exchange—where giving becomes sacrifice, and sacrifice becomes a transaction in the realm of the Spirit.

Sacrificial giving is not about the size of what is given, but the weight it carries in obedience, surrender, and spiritual significance. Sacrifice births covenants, shifts destinies, and alters spiritual verdicts. On this altar, God does not merely receive the gift; He responds to the giver.

From Offering to Sacrifice There are levels to giving:

- An offering is what you give in honor or gratitude.
- A sacrifice is what you give in obedience, often under tension or pressure.
- A dangerous gift is what you give to provoke divine reversal or settle matters in the spirit.

Each level speaks a different language in the courts of heaven. The altar of exchange is built when what you give touches your identity, your future, or your comfort zone. It is no longer about transaction; it is about covenant.

Abraham and Isaac: The Sacrifice That Spoke (Genesis 22)

In Genesis 22, Abraham was not asked for money. He was asked for his future—his son. And yet, in radical obedience, he journeyed to the mountain with Isaac, prepared an altar, and lifted the knife.

Though God intervened and provided a ram, Abraham's obedience created something irreversible: a covenant of multiplication and dominion. "Because you have done this…" was the divine statement that followed. His giving redefined his lineage.

Sometimes the altar is not built for God to take; it is built for God to see how far you are willing to go.

David at the Threshing Floor: Sacrifice to Stop a Plague (2 Samuel 24:24–25)

After a costly mistake, David found himself interceding to stop a plague ravaging his people. He approached Araunah to purchase a threshing floor to build an altar. Araunah offered it freely, but David refused.

"I will not offer to the Lord that which costs me nothing."

David paid the full price. And when the altar was built and the offering laid, the plague was stopped. His sacrifice became intercession. His giving shifted divine judgment.

Some battles are not silenced by prayer or fasting alone; they are silenced by sacrificial obedience on an altar of exchange.

The Altar as Legal Ground An altar is not just a place; it is a legal ground in the spirit. When a sacrifice is placed on an altar under divine instruction:

- Heaven records it.
- Angels are dispatched.
- Patterns are interrupted.
- Covenants are initiated or renewed.

Sacrificial giving opens portals that regular prayer cannot. It builds altars that speak when words run dry.

The altar of exchange reveals the supernatural power of sacrifice. It is the ground upon which spiritual transactions are made; transactions that provoke covenant, interrupt judgment, or shift verdicts. Whether seen in Abraham's obedience, David's costly offering, or the Moabite king's dark sacrifice, the principle remains: what touches your future touches the spirit realm. Giving at this level is warfare; it rewrites outcomes and brings divine attention. The altar becomes a courtroom, and your sacrifice becomes your evidence. When engaged by revelation, it is one of the most powerful weapons in the believer's arsenal.

Giving That Births Solutions and Breaks Resistance Giving has a mysterious way of opening prophetic portals, provoking divine remembrance, and unlocking answers no strategy, negotiation, or endurance could produce. It is not merely about responding to lack; it is often about confronting resistance, birthing escape routes, and overriding systems designed to block progress.

There are seasons when prayer has been offered, integrity maintained, and effort exhausted—yet movement remains stalled. In such moments, giving, when led by divine instruction, enters as reinforcement. It does not replace prayer; it strengthens it. It does not contradict faith; it gives faith a voice in the unseen realm.

What leaves your hand in obedience can create leverage in the spirit.

Dorcas: Giving Her Way Out of Death In Acts 9:36–41, Dorcas (also called Tabitha) stands as one of the clearest demonstrations of giving that births an impossible solution. She was known for quiet generosity—clothing widows, serving without publicity, and expecting no return. Her giving built a memorial long before crisis arrived.

When she died, her community refused to accept the finality of death. They did not appeal to her status or title; they presented evidence of her giving. The widows stood weeping, holding the garments she had made. Her seed spoke when her voice was silent.

Peter prayed, and Dorcas was restored to life.

Her giving interrupted death's authority.

Giving can provoke divine remembrance that overrides natural order.

The Shunammite Woman: Giving Into Legacy In 2 Kings 4, the Shunammite woman did not give because she lacked; she gave because she perceived. She recognized the grace on Elisha's life and built a room for him. There was no request, no manipulation, no transactional expectation.

Yet her discernment-driven generosity unlocked what wealth could not buy: a son. Later, when that son died, the same prophetic relationship her giving activated became the channel for resurrection.

Her gift did not merely open a womb; it preserved a legacy.

Giving from perception carries resurrection power.

Solomon: Giving That Provoked Divine Wisdom When Solomon offered a thousand burnt offerings (1 Kings 3), there was no visible crisis demanding a solution. But his seed provoked an encounter. That night, God appeared to him in a dream and said, "Ask what I shall give you."

Solomon's giving invited divine intelligence into the complexity of leadership. What followed was wisdom that redefined governance, prosperity that astonished nations, and stability that secured Israel's future.

Some solutions are not responses to problems; they are preparations for responsibility.

Cornelius: Giving That Opened the Gate of Salvation Cornelius did not know he had a problem. Yet Acts 10 tells us that his prayers and his alms ascended as a memorial before God. Heaven responded—not with money or promotion, but with access.

Peter was sent to his house, and Cornelius became the entry point through which the Gentile world received salvation. His giving unlocked a solution far larger than his personal life; it shifted redemptive history.

Giving can open doors you did not know existed.

The Widow of Zarephath: Giving That Broke Economic Warfare The widow of Zarephath in 1 Kings 17 was not merely poor; she was living under economic warfare induced by drought. Her giving was not convenient; it was prophetic. She gave her last meal under instruction, and the embargo over her household was broken.

The jar did not run dry. The oil did not fail.

Her seed dismantled scarcity.

Giving can break economic resistance where labor and planning fail.

A Personal Testimony: Giving That Created an Escape Route I was in a very deep and difficult battle during my undergraduate years at Ogun State University, where I studied Mathematics. At the time, I was in my 200 level—young in the faith, bold, and admittedly immature. I was a committed Christian, but I was also confrontational. On several occasions, I challenged excesses openly and even preached in class. My zeal lacked wisdom, and it made me a target.

About three lecturers took issue—not with my academic ability, but with my profession of faith. Their resistance was subtle at first, then strategic. I failed multiple courses taught by them, across both semesters. Mathematics courses are sequential; each class is a prerequisite for the next. Failing those courses effectively blocked my academic progression.

They sent intermediaries to advise me to "do normal." That phrase was not academic; it was ideological. It meant comply. I refused.

Their tactics escalated. Anytime I traveled for the Holy Ghost Service at Redemption Camp, they would schedule impromptu mandatory classes and tests. I would return to campus already marked absent. I could not beg for make-ups without submitting to their conditions, and I refused to place myself at the mercy of compromise.

I prayed. I fasted. I stood my ground.

But nothing shifted.

One day, while praying, I received a clear leading—not to pray more, but to give. It was not money. It was symbolic.

At that time, Pastor E. A. Adeboye often ministered wearing Adire—a traditional fabric unique to Abeokuta. I went and bought a ready-made Adire top. It was not fabric; it was a sewn garment. I sowed it intentionally, as both a birthday gift and a seed of warfare.

My prayer was simple: *"Father, as clothing covers nakedness, cover my shame in this battle."*

The academic attack I faced was not due to incompetence; it was designed to expose me publicly because of my faith. Students had already been sent to warn me to stop attending Redemption Camp and to stop following Adeboye. That instruction was specific and non-negotiable. I was not following a man; I was following Christ. But the pressure was real.

I gave the seed on a Friday.

The following week, after the weekend, I returned to campus—and a crisis erupted only in the Mathematics Department. All the lecturers who had opposed me were dismissed. The department was left with only the Head of Department and one other full-time lecturer.

An emergency meeting was called.

Because of my failed courses, I should not have been eligible to proceed to 300 level. But due to the sudden staffing collapse, visiting professors were arranged from the University of Ife (now Obafemi Awolowo University). These professors would only teach 300-level courses on weekends.

The HOD signed blank registration forms and instructed us to register for the classes we needed.

That signature became my escape route.

I registered for the failed 200-level courses still taught during the week—and simultaneously registered for the 300-level courses taught on weekends. By the time the political conflict between the dismissed lecturers and the state government was resolved, I was already in my final year.

I defended my project successfully.

One of the reinstated lecturers—who had been part of my ordeal—was present during the defense. As I walked out, he followed me and said:

"That was a good presentation… but do you know you are not graduating?"

I said nothing.

I had learned there are people you do not fight.

What matters—and must be said clearly—is this: I passed every single course. The failed 200-level courses. The regular 300-level courses.

There was no academic deficiency—only spiritual resistance.

The only thing I did differently was give.

That seed did not change their hearts. It changed the terrain.

Nobody can convince me otherwise. The precision of the outcome—the timing, the isolation of the department, the sequence of events—was too exact. That giving created a path solution, dismantled resistance, and preserved my destiny without confrontation.

Sometimes, God does not remove the enemy. He removes their leverage.

And sometimes, the weapon that does it is not prayer alone, but a seed assigned for warfare.

When Giving Becomes Warfare – The Law of Strategic Sacrifice One of the most sobering truths in spiritual warfare is that a battle can be initiated by God and still be altered by spiritual intelligence on the opposing side. This is precisely what happened in the war against Moab.

Israel, Judah, and Edom did not go to war on a whim. This campaign was not born out of ambition, revenge, or political maneuvering. God Himself authorized the fight. Through prophetic instruction, the coalition was assured of victory. Strategically, everything aligned. Militarily, Moab was outmatched. City after city fell. The enemy was cornered. From every visible angle, the outcome was settled.

Yet spiritual warfare is never decided by visibility alone.

As the Moabite king watched his defenses collapse and his forces disintegrate, he recognized a reality many believers overlook: there are moments when conventional strategy no longer works, and only spiritual transaction can alter outcomes. With no military escape and no diplomatic leverage left, he turned to the unseen realm—not in repentance, but in calculation.

In a public, deliberate, and horrifying act, the king took his firstborn son—the heir to his throne, the carrier of his legacy, the future of his lineage—and sacrificed him on the city wall in full view of both armies. This was not an emotional breakdown. It was not desperation alone. It was a conscious engagement of spiritual law.

That son represented continuity, authority, inheritance, and posterity. By offering him, the king did not merely give a life; he gave his future.

Scripture records that immediately after this sacrifice, "there was great indignation against Israel." The atmosphere shifted. Momentum changed. The coalition withdrew. The war ended—not because Moab suddenly became stronger, but because the spiritual climate had been altered.

This is the unsettling lesson: The offering worked.

God did not revoke His integrity. He did not suddenly favor Moab. But He honors principles, even when they are engaged by ungodly hands. The spiritual realm operates on laws, not sentiment. When a law is activated, it produces an outcome, regardless of who initiates it.

This is why this story must be handled with sobriety. The Moabite king was ungodly, but he was spiritually intelligent. He understood that sacrifice speaks, that altars create legal shifts, and that certain offerings generate spiritual force capable of interrupting even divinely authorized momentum.

Israel was not defeated by Moab's army. They were halted by a transaction they did not counter-discern.

This moment exposes a hard truth many believers resist: victory is not sustained by calling alone, but by continued spiritual alignment and discernment. God ordered the battle, but the atmosphere was hijacked through an extreme and dark offering. The sacrifice became an indignation, a force that altered engagement rules in the unseen realm.

This is not an endorsement of ungodly sacrifice. It is a warning.

If the kingdom of darkness understands how to use giving, at great personal cost, to shift outcomes, then believers must awaken to the reality that what we are willing to give up, and how we give, matters deeply in warfare. Many lose battles not because God is absent, but because the enemy is more intentional, more costly, and more strategic in how they engage spiritual laws.

This is the law of strategic sacrifice. And it explains why some battles do not end where they began, even when God authorized the fight.

Why Didn't God Counter It? This battle was initiated by God. Victory was guaranteed. The enemies of Israel were being defeated. But when the Moabite king made that sacrificial move, something shifted in the atmosphere.

God did not counter the sacrifice, not because He approved of it, but because He is bound by His integrity to honor spiritual laws, even when engaged by the ungodly.

Here's why: God is just, not partial. He does not break principles, even for His people. He embodies them.

This was not about righteousness; it was about legal authority in the spiritual realm. The Moabite king, though pagan, tapped into a spiritual law of ultimate sacrifice. And that level of sacrifice created a spiritual atmosphere that God, in His justice and integrity, could not ignore.

If God were to overlook that offering, He would violate the very laws that govern both justice and sacrifice. The power of a firstborn sacrifice, while dark in origin, mirrored something deeply embedded in divine structure: the principle of atonement and ultimate offering. And in the court of heaven, principles often trump personalities.

The Integrity of Principle in Divine Justice God does not operate like men. He does not adjust principles for convenience. While human beings evaluate outcomes by emotions and loyalty, God evaluates by alignment and authority.

In this instance, the Moabite king offered something so weighty that it provoked a spiritual indignation, not necessarily from God, but from the spiritual realm itself. That indignation created a legal resistance that Israel could not penetrate, not even with divine backing, because a higher spiritual law had been activated.

You can be ungodly and still be spiritually intelligent.

Spiritual intelligence is about understanding how realms operate, not about moral standing.

The king of Moab understood the terrain he was fighting in. When he saw no natural escape, he engaged the ultimate spiritual leverage: sacrifice. And it worked.

Not because it pleased God. But because it aligned with an ancient principle that governs outcomes when all else fails.

Why Many Christians Still Lose This is where many believers falter. They underestimate the spiritual intelligence of their enemies. They assume that because a battle is "God-ordained," victory is guaranteed regardless of their personal positioning, obedience, or engagement of divine laws.

But spiritual warfare is not just about being on the right side. It's about operating under divine intelligence.

The Moabite king outmaneuvered Israel, not by might, but by understanding spiritual protocols. He engaged a law that invoked spiritual force, and in doing so, created a shift so violent that God, in His integrity, allowed the battle to end.

The Double-Edged Nature of Giving Giving, when understood through this lens, is not charity; it is legislation in the spirit.

It can be light or dark. Godly or demonic. But its effectiveness lies in the weight of what is given and the realm it is offered into.

When you give sacrificially, you are not just releasing a seed. You are making a legal demand on a realm, and that realm must respond according to its governing principles.

Sacrifice speaks where words fail. Sacrifice interrupts cycles. Sacrifice shifts atmospheres, whether you are on the mountain of God or standing on the wall of Moab.

This is the law of strategic sacrifice.

A Call to Strategic Sacrifice: Activating Giving as a Weapon Not all giving is warfare. Not all sacrifice is strategic. But when guided by revelation, giving becomes a spiritual weapon that can settle disputes in the courts of heaven and provoke divine intervention on earth.

In spiritual warfare, there are moments when prayer, fasting, or even declarations reach their limits, not because they are weak, but because the matter at hand requires a weightier engagement. At those moments, the Spirit of God will often stir you to give something that costs you. It may be your time, your treasure, or even your position. Whatever it is, strategic giving is surgical. It targets a stronghold with precision and breaks through barriers that words alone cannot penetrate.

Sacrifice Is Not Random—It Is Revealed The power of a strategic sacrifice is not in its emotional weight, but in its alignment with divine instruction. Abraham's offering of Isaac was not merely radical; it was ordered. God told him what, where, and how to sacrifice. That obedience unlocked a generational covenant (Genesis 22:16–18).

David once faced a plague that was destroying Israel. The solution was not another meeting or even another fast. It was a sacrifice: "I will not offer to the Lord that which costs me nothing" (2 Samuel 24:24). That offering stopped the plague.

Strategic giving is not about the amount; it's about the assignment.

What Makes a Sacrifice Strategic?

1. It is prompted by revelation, not routine.
2. It is timed, not random; there's a window where the sacrifice speaks loudest.
3. It is specific—not everything qualifies as a sacrifice; it must cost you.

4. It is aimed—at a spiritual need, battle, or transaction.

The Moabite king, though wicked, understood the timing and targeting of sacrifice. His son's death spoke to the spiritual realm in a way that disrupted Israel's momentum.

Should we follow his example? No. But we must learn the principle.

The kingdom of darkness understands sacrifice and doesn't hesitate to use it. The kingdom of God requires it—but often finds believers unwilling, hesitant, or ignorant of its power.

If you won't offer what matters to you, don't expect realms to move.

Giving as a Weapon When led by God, giving is not a loss; it's a declaration of war. It's saying: *I refuse to let the enemy win because I withhold what heaven needs to authorize my victory.*

In moments of strategic warfare, your seed becomes a sword, your offering becomes an altar, and your obedience becomes an ordinance that heaven honors.

In battles where delay, oppression, or stagnation has become chronic, ask:

- Is there a sacrifice God is prompting me to make?
- Have I tried everything except what costs me?
- Is this a battle that requires a strategic offering to settle it once and for all?

The Voice of Sacrifice The voice of sacrifice is often louder than the voice of complaint.

- God may not need your money, but He requires your obedience through it. That obedience may open a door, shift a verdict, or silence an accuser.
- We must graduate from emotional giving to strategic sacrifice. We must move from impulsive sowing to revelatory giving. We must stop giving for applause and start giving for access.
- And when we do, we'll find that giving is not just a gesture; it is a governance tool. One that, when used under divine instruction, can secure victories no enemy can reverse.

The Root of Redemption: Giving as a Legal Exchange The greatest warfare ever waged was not fought with swords, angels, or armies; it was fought on a cross. And the most potent weapon in that battle was a gift.

The root of salvation is a transaction: God gave.

John 3:16 declares it plainly: “For God so loved the world that He gave…” This is not poetic; it is legal. Salvation was not a rescue by sentiment. It was a divine exchange. The righteous for the unrighteous. The holy for the defiled. The innocent for the guilty. At the center of the gospel is the principle of strategic giving.

Jesus on the cross was not a victim of Roman violence; He was the sacrificial seed in the most powerful legal exchange of all time. The cross was not a defeat; it was a courtroom transaction that satisfied the justice of heaven and forever altered the destiny of man.

Isaiah 53 reveals the legal framework of this divine transaction: *“The chastisement for our peace was upon Him, and by His stripes we are healed...”*

This was not random suffering. It was intentional substitution. He took so we could receive. He gave so we could become.

In this light, giving is not a religious activity; it is a legal act that can be used in warfare. When we give in obedience and alignment, we engage the same laws that governed the cross. We do not purchase grace—grace is not for sale—but we position ourselves within the judicial system of God's Kingdom to receive what grace freely provides.

There are dimensions of breakthrough, favor, and access that are not earned, but they are activated through sacrificial alignment. Giving is one such activation.

Like the cross, sacrificial giving speaks in realms where words fail. It settles accusations, silences resistance, and opens gates that could never be unlocked by human effort alone. When your giving echoes heaven's pattern, you trigger heaven's response.

So, whether you are facing a battle in your mind, your finances, your ministry, or your family—remember this: Victory is not just won by might or by power; it is often secured by a well-placed sacrifice.

Give when God says give. Give what He says to give. And give with the understanding that you are not losing; you are legislating.

Chapter 5

Silence is a Weapon of War

Silence: The Overlooked Weapon of Warfare

One of the most underestimated but powerful tools in spiritual warfare is silence. Like giving, silence is something we engage in daily, intentionally or unintentionally. But silence is far more than the absence of speech; it is a multi-purpose spiritual weapon that can shape outcomes across all realms of battle: internal (soul), human-to-human, and spiritual (invisible conflict). While it may seem passive, strategic silence is deeply tactical. It is never neutral; it either works for you or against you, depending on how and when it is used.

Many ignore silence in the heat of warfare because it doesn't feel like action. It doesn’t shout. It doesn’t command attention. Yet its power is precisely found in its quiet precision. It requires more emotional discipline, discernment, and maturity than most other spiritual tools. Silence is often dismissed because it lacks immediate visibility, but when rightly employed, it becomes an instrument of preservation, provocation, revelation, and even divine intervention.

Silence is not merely a personal preference or a temperament trait; it is a learned posture that demands spiritual intelligence. It’s a weapon that cuts deeper than words when wielded rightly and more dangerously when misused. To understand how silence functions as a weapon, we must first understand its nature and how it fits within the broader framework of communication.

Silence and the Nature of Communication

Communication is the transmission of information, not just through words, but through tone, posture, gesture, timing, expression, and intention. According to communication theory, only 7% of communication is verbal. The remaining

93% is non-verbal, comprised of body language, facial expressions, eye contact, and tone of voice.

In that context, true silence is more than withholding speech. It is a holistic disengagement from all forms of expressive communication, verbal and non-verbal. Strategic silence is not the same as emotional withdrawal, passive-aggressive behavior, or stoic repression. It is an intentional stance of disengagement from unnecessary dialogue, premature confrontation, or emotionally driven reactions, for the purpose of warfare, clarity, or divine instruction.

Consider this: even silence sends a message.

- A delay in response can signal wisdom, or fear.
- A refusal to speak can demonstrate strength, or cowardice.
- A calm demeanor in chaos can intimidate an enemy more than loud declarations.

Therefore, the quality of silence matters. Carnal silence can be manipulative, rooted in pride, fear, or emotional immaturity. But spiritual silence is intentional, intelligent, and often prophetic. It allows a person to observe, perceive, and prepare before acting. It builds resistance in the soul while disarming the enemy.

The Bible is filled with moments where silence wasn't just absence; it was strategy.

The Faculty of Speech — Life and Death in the Tongue

"Death and life are in the power of the tongue, and they that love it shall eat the fruit thereof." — Proverbs 18:21

Speech is one of the most powerful faculties entrusted to humanity. It is not merely a tool for expression; it is an instrument of creation, alignment, destruction, and warfare. Words are not neutral. They carry authority, intention, and consequence. In both the natural and spiritual realms, what is spoken activates outcomes, establishes agreements, and opens or closes doors.

From the beginning, Scripture reveals that speech governs reality. God created by speaking. Light did not appear until it was spoken into existence. Likewise, human beings, made in the image of God, were entrusted with the faculty of speech as a delegated authority. This is why words do not simply describe reality; they participate in shaping it.

The fall of humanity did not occur through disobedience alone. It began with conversation.

Eve did not eat the fruit in silence. She engaged in dialogue. The serpent did not force rebellion; he initiated discussion. He weaponized speech by questioning God's word, reframing truth, and introducing doubt through carefully crafted conversation. The first battlefield was not behavior; it was communication. The serpent understood that if he could control the dialogue, he could redirect destiny.

This reveals a sobering truth: speech is often the entry point of defeat.

In warfare, the tongue functions both as a sword and a snare. It can defend truth or expose vulnerability. It can establish authority or surrender it. Words can end battles, but they can also ignite them. Many conflicts escalate not because of actions, but because of unmanaged speech. Likewise, many victories are delayed not because of lack of prayer, but because of premature or excessive talking.

You can lose by saying too much.

Loose speech leaks intelligence. Over-explaining weakens authority. Reacting verbally in moments of provocation often hands control to the enemy. Words spoken in anger, fear, pride, or emotional instability can undo years of discipline and alignment. Once released, words cannot be retrieved. They become witnesses in both human and spiritual courts.

Yet you can also lose by saying too little. Silence without discernment can be just as dangerous as reckless speech. There are moments when silence is wisdom, but there are also moments when silence becomes consent, avoidance, or fear. Withholding truth when God requires declaration is not humility; it is disobedience. Silence that ignores injustice, suppresses instruction, or avoids responsibility can allow destruction to advance unchecked.

This is why silence cannot be governed by temperament or emotion. It must be governed by discernment.

The same tongue that can destroy can also deliver. The same mouth that can betray can also bless. The issue is not speech versus silence; it is timing, instruction, and maturity. Warfare demands the ability to know when to speak and when to restrain speech. Without that discernment, both silence and speech become liabilities.

The faculty of speech is powerful because it sits at the intersection of spirit, soul, and body. When aligned with God, it becomes a weapon of victory. When misaligned, it becomes a tool of defeat. Mastery in warfare requires learning not just how to speak, but when to be silent, and why.

In the next section, we will confront the misuse of silence and expose how malice, manipulation, and immaturity distort what should be a strategic weapon into a source of harm.

Misused Silence: Malice, Manipulation, and Immaturity

Before silence can be used as a weapon of spiritual intelligence, its counterfeits must be exposed.

Not all silence is golden.

Not every silent posture is rooted in wisdom, strategy, or discernment. Some forms of silence are carnal, destructive, and manipulative, designed to control, confuse, or conceal. These distorted versions of silence masquerade as spiritual maturity but are, in truth, emotional sabotage in disguise.

Silence can be a strategic weapon only when it is governed by purity of motive and emotional maturity.

But when misused, silence becomes a tool of the flesh—an act of rebellion, not reverence.

Common Forms of Misused Silence:

1. **Punitive Silence (The Weapon of Control)** This is silence used as punishment. It is deployed to withhold attention, affection, or clarity until the other person feels uncomfortable enough to bend or break. It's not rooted in wisdom; it's about power. This is not the silence of a wise warrior; it is the tantrum of an emotionally insecure soul.
2. **Passive-Aggressive Spirituality** Some use silence to appear spiritually composed, while internally seething with pride, judgment, or bitterness. This version of silence is often justified as "keeping peace," when in reality, it's a silent war that denies resolution. It is a lie wrapped in piety.
3. **Emotional Withdrawal as Avoidance** In conflict or tension, silence can be used to escape accountability. The person checks out emotionally but stays physically present, creating confusion and emotional

abandonment. Withdrawal is not wisdom; it is often fear pretending to be restraint.

4. **Silence as a Mirror of Superiority** Silence that leaks contempt, disdain, or pride is not spiritual; it is a declaration of superiority without saying a word. This kind of silence seeks to diminish the other person's voice, leaving them feeling unheard, unworthy, or dismissed. Silence must never be used as a pedestal.

The Dangers of Manipulative Silence

- It preys on the emotionally vulnerable: Misused silence is especially harmful to those who crave affirmation, clarity, or connection. The withholding of words becomes a tool to trigger fear, anxiety, or desperation.
- It communicates confusion: Unlike strategic silence, which clarifies and calms, manipulative silence distorts communication and leaves others guessing. It often prolongs conflict instead of resolving it. •
- It sabotages intimacy: In relationships—whether personal, spiritual, or professional—manipulative silence creates walls instead of bridges. It turns connection into a competition for power.

Spiritual warfare requires emotional intelligence. Silence must be governed by a sanctified motive, not a self-serving one. Before you reach for the weapon of silence, examine the intent of your heart. Is it to preserve peace or provoke pain? Is it to seek clarity or create confusion?

Strategic Silence: Clarity, Alignment, and Revelation

There is a time to speak, and there is a time to be silent. But strategic silence is not simply the absence of speech; it is the intentional withdrawal of verbal response for a higher spiritual and tactical purpose. In the realm of spiritual warfare, silence is not a void. It is a posture. It is not passive; it is powerful. Just as a soldier may crouch or hide before a targeted strike, the believer too must learn when to step back, not out of fear, but in obedience to a higher instruction. Ecclesiastes 3:7 reminds us, "There is a time to keep silence, and a time to speak." Mastering this balance is not instinctive; it must be learned.

Strategic silence creates space for divine intelligence to surface. It suspends the demands of the soul long enough for the spirit to lead. It silences the noise of external voices and internal reasoning to allow clarity, instruction, and divine timing to emerge. Psalm 46:10 commands, "Be still, and know that I am God." This stillness is not inactivity; it is the quieting of the soul so that spiritual knowledge may be accessed. It is in this stillness that wisdom is whispered, strategies are unfolded, and divine timing is aligned.

David captured this beautifully in Psalm 131:2 when he said, "But I have calmed and quieted my soul, like a weaned child with its mother; like a weaned child is my soul within me." This imagery is profound. A weaned child is not screaming for milk. It is resting in trust. It is not driven by immediate need, but by presence and connection. Strategic silence mirrors this—we are not silent because we have nothing to say, but because we choose to let God's voice override our own. Silence, in this sense, becomes the language of spiritual maturity.

In seasons of warfare, confusion often clouds judgment. The louder the battle, the more tempting it becomes to speak hastily, defend ourselves prematurely, or reveal insights too soon. But in such moments, noise confuses; silence clarifies. The practice of silence allows us to discern the true origin of the battle—is it self-inflicted, demonically orchestrated, divinely initiated, or relationally triggered? That distinction is crucial, because each requires a different response. Silence buys time for this discernment.

Silence also serves as a shield. It prevents the premature exposure of revelation. Some battles escalate because insight is shared too early or with the wrong audience. Silence becomes a wall that guards what is sacred until it is time to act. Spiritual intelligence often requires silence as its foundation. Revelation not yet fully formed must be protected in the womb of silence, lest it be aborted by misunderstanding or opposition.

I once went through a season that tested this truth in the deepest way. It was a time of relentless warfare: unrelenting pressure, misunderstanding, spiritual dryness, and emotional exhaustion. I prayed every kind of prayer I knew. I sowed sacrificial seeds. I fasted. I declared Scripture. And yet, the battle would not shift. In desperation, I sought the Lord for answers. But instead of detailed instructions, He gave me only one verse: "Be still and know that I am God" (Psalm 46:10). That was it. No new prophecy. No fresh word. Just that.

At first, I thought "being still" meant doing nothing externally. But the Lord showed me that stillness must first happen internally. I was obeying outwardly, but my inner world was noisy. I was negotiating, explaining, venting, and rehearsing possibilities in my head. There was no stillness. Just mental chaos hidden behind a silent mouth.

So I took a radical step. I registered for a 3-day silent retreat at the Ignatius House, a Jesuit retreat center in Sandy Springs, Georgia. It was a beautiful environment, designed for solitude and contemplation. The rules were strict: no talking, no phones, no interaction. I didn't realize how loud I truly was until I got there. On the first night, I began to sing to myself in the room—old habits die hard. Minutes later, I heard a gentle knock on my door and saw a note slid underneath. It simply read: "Please be quiet."

That one sentence rebuked me. It exposed the noise I was still carrying, even in silence. For the first two days, I struggled. My internal dialogue was nonstop. I was trying to obey, but my soul refused to sit down. I realized that I had never truly practiced being still. I had been surviving through noise. But on the third day, something shifted. A deep quiet began to settle in my spirit. For the first time, I saw how my internal chaos had blocked divine instruction. I saw how many decisions I had made out of noise rather than clarity. I saw how often I had mistaken movement for obedience.

That retreat was not just restful; it was revelatory. I realized that silence is not a reaction; it is a strategy. It is not empty space; it is the training ground of the soul. I haven't returned to that retreat center yet—but writing this section reminds me that it's time. Silence must be revisited. It must be practiced. It must be honored. Because silence is a spiritual weapon that only works when it is anchored in trust and obedience.

In spiritual warfare, not every moment is a speaking moment. Not every battle requires a reply. Not every accusation deserves an answer. Not every revelation must be shared immediately. Strategic silence teaches us restraint. And in that restraint, we find alignment, strength, and power.

Silence and Spiritual Intelligence

Wars are won by intelligence, not noise.

The greatest victories, whether in natural or spiritual warfare, are not determined by how loud the battle cry is, but by how precise the strategy is. The most effective soldiers are not always the most visible; they are the most informed. In this regard, silence is not weakness; it is wisdom in disguise. True warriors understand that not everything must be said, and not every move must be explained.

Information control is warfare.

This is one of the foundational principles of spiritual intelligence. The one who controls information—what is said, when it is said, and to whom it is said—controls the battlefield. The enemy cannot counter what he cannot anticipate. This is why intelligence agencies in the natural world operate in silence. They gather data quietly. They act covertly. They preserve the element of surprise. In like manner, spiritual intelligence is preserved through discretion.

Loose lips create unnecessary casualties.

Many believers lose battles not because they lack power, but because they lack discipline with their words. Premature announcements, careless conversations, and emotionally driven disclosures can sabotage divine strategies. Judas Iscariot needed only a kiss to betray Jesus; he had already been informed. Information leakage in the spirit realm is just as dangerous as on a battlefield. Many destinies have been ambushed by what was prematurely spoken.

Silence preserves advantage. To preserve advantage in warfare, one must understand timing and restraint. Even Jesus withheld certain truths from the public, saying, *"I have many more things to say to you, but you cannot bear them now"* (John 16:12, NLT). Silence is not always secrecy; it is often mercy. By choosing when and how to speak, you avoid overwhelming others, provoking unnecessary resistance, or derailing divine timing. Not every silence is a delay; some silences are divine shields.

This is why intelligence agencies value secrecy.

Governments understand that the success of national defense often depends on silence. Codes, encryption, and classified operations exist to keep adversaries in the dark. The same principle applies to spiritual warfare. God does not reveal His entire plan at once, and neither should you. Revelation is often progressive, given in pieces to preserve safety, obedience, and trust.

The spirit realm operates the same way.

When Daniel prayed and fasted, the answer was dispatched immediately, but spiritual resistance delayed it (Daniel 10). If Daniel had spoken too soon or stopped too early, he might have forfeited the revelation. There is a rhythm to revelation that requires spiritual intelligence to manage. What you know in the spirit must be protected until the time of its manifestation.

Silence is not inactivity. It is information management.

There is a common misconception that silence means passivity. In truth, spiritual silence is an active discipline. It is the management of information, the concealment of strategies, and the preservation of purpose. It is the intentional withholding of speech not out of fear, but out of understanding. In the realm of spiritual intelligence, silence is not empty; it is encrypted.

Jesus Before His Accusers – Silence as Supreme Spiritual Intelligence

"He was oppressed and treated harshly, yet he never said a word. He was led like a lamb to the slaughter. And as a sheep is silent before the shearers, He did not open his mouth." — Isaiah 53:7, NLT

Jesus, the Word made flesh, knew precisely when not to speak.

In the climactic moment of His earthly assignment, surrounded by false accusations, political manipulation, and religious hypocrisy, Jesus chose silence. Before Pilate, before Herod, and even before the religious leaders who plotted His death, He displayed a level of strategic restraint that transcended human impulse and legal defense. His silence was not passivity. It was not fear. It was power under absolute control.

In warfare, silence is often mistaken for weakness. But in the courtroom of divine justice, silence can signal dominance. Jesus, who had all authority in heaven and on earth, did not need to prove innocence to those whose motives were corrupted. He could have called down legions of angels or silenced His accusers with a word. Yet He allowed the accusations to pile up without a single rebuttal, because He was not fighting for vindication. He was executing a divine exchange.

This moment teaches us something profound: spiritual intelligence discerns the difference between when to defend and when to surrender, not in defeat, but in alignment. Jesus' silence was not merely a tactic; it was an alignment with prophecy, with timing, and with the will of the Father. Every word He did not say fulfilled Scripture. Every silence carried weight in heaven.

There is a level of maturity where your silence is louder than argument. It becomes your sword, not your absence. The maturity to refrain from speech, even when misunderstood, falsely accused, or under pressure, is evidence of inner dominance. Jesus was not confused about His identity. He knew who He was, and that confidence allowed Him to stay silent when lesser men would have pleaded.

This silence broke legal and spiritual barriers. By refusing to participate in the corrupt systems that sought to entrap Him with words, He maintained spiritual leverage. His silence shut the mouths of mockers and fulfilled the requirement of the sacrificial Lamb—spotless, undefended, surrendered.

Silence, when anchored in purpose, becomes a declaration. It says: I don't need to argue when the outcome is already decided. It resists provocation, denies the enemy access to unnecessary intel, and maintains spiritual superiority. This is not the silence of avoidance; it is the silence of alignment.

In our own battles, especially where reputations, decisions, or leadership are at stake, we must learn this discipline. Not all accusations require an answer. Not every attack needs a defense. Sometimes, silence is the most eloquent response a mature spirit can offer.

When you know heaven has spoken, silence becomes your statement of trust.

When to Engage Silence in Warfare

There is a time to speak, and there is a time when silence is not just golden, but godly. In spiritual warfare, silence is not an absence of strategy; it is the strategy. Knowing when to engage silence can be the difference between spiritual victory and unnecessary defeat. Just as swords are not drawn in every battle, words must not be released in every moment. Silence can be a shield, a signal, or a supernatural code that confuses the enemy and aligns you with divine timing.

Silence is strategic when the enemy is stronger or more influential. When David fled from Saul, he chose silence over accusation. He did not try to out-argue or out-power the reigning king. Instead, he allowed his restraint to testify. Speaking out prematurely, especially in front of those who are more established or influential, can expose you to unnecessary backlash. Sometimes, silence is the only safe response when the odds are stacked against you. A roar in the wrong arena can become an echo of defeat.

Silence is wise when you are falsely accused. Jesus modeled this on trial before His crucifixion. He answered not a word when Pilate, Herod, and the high priests hurled false accusations. In moments of misrepresentation, silence allows the dust of emotion to settle and the truth to rise. Defensiveness can sound like guilt. But silence, when led by discernment, speaks volumes. Time and fruit will vindicate the righteous.

Silence is necessary when dealing with manipulative or fox-like personalities. Jesus referred to Herod as "that fox" (Luke 13:32). When confronted by crafty, manipulative individuals, every word can become ammunition in the hands of the enemy. Engaging such personalities verbally often results in entrapment or twisted narratives. Strategic silence is not fear; it is warfare intelligence. It disarms those who feed on response and forces them to wrestle with their own emptiness.

Silence is protective during seasons of transition. Transition is a delicate corridor between endings and beginnings. It is the place where clarity is still forming and decisions are being tested. Talking too much in transition can expose fragile ideas, unfinished instructions, or misaligned plans. Silence protects the incubating season from contamination. Not every seed should be spoken before it takes root.

Silence is vital when revelation must be protected. Many divine instructions are aborted because they are prematurely announced. Joseph's dream drew unnecessary warfare when it was shared before its time. Divine revelation thrives in silence. Like Mary, who "pondered these things in her heart" (Luke 2:19), we must learn to guard spiritual downloads until their appointed time of manifestation. The womb of revelation requires the atmosphere of secrecy.

Silence is wise when clarity has not yet formed. Speaking without clarity is like shooting an arrow in the dark; it may hurt others or sabotage your path. In seasons of confusion, it is better to say nothing than to say something you cannot retrieve. Silence buys time. Time exposes truth. Delaying speech until divine understanding emerges is a mark of maturity and humility.

Silence and Spiritual Intelligence Wars are won by intelligence, not noise.

The greatest victories, whether in natural or spiritual warfare, are not determined by how loud the battle cry is, but by how precise the strategy is. The most effective soldiers are not always the most visible; they are the most informed. In this regard, silence is not weakness; it is wisdom in disguise. True warriors understand that not everything must be said, and not every move must be explained.

Information control is warfare.

This is one of the foundational principles of spiritual intelligence. The one who controls information—what is said, when it is said, and to whom it is said—controls the battlefield. The enemy cannot counter what he cannot anticipate. This is why intelligence agencies in the natural world operate in silence. They gather data quietly. They act covertly. They preserve the element of surprise. In like manner, spiritual intelligence is preserved through discretion.

Loose lips create unnecessary casualties.

Many believers lose battles not because they lack power, but because they lack discipline with their words. Premature announcements, careless conversations, and emotionally driven disclosures can sabotage divine strategies. Judas Iscariot needed only a kiss to betray Jesus; he had already been informed. Information leakage in the spirit realm is just as dangerous as on a battlefield. Many destinies have been ambushed by what was prematurely spoken.

Silence preserves advantage. To preserve advantage in warfare, one must understand timing and restraint. Even Jesus withheld certain truths from the public, saying, "I have many more things to say to you, but you cannot bear them now" (John 16:12, NLT). Silence is not always secrecy; it is often mercy. By choosing when and how to speak, you avoid overwhelming others, provoking unnecessary resistance, or derailing divine timing. Not every silence is a delay; some silences are divine shields.

This is why intelligence agencies value secrecy.

Governments understand that the success of national defense often depends on silence. Codes, encryption, and classified operations exist to keep adversaries in the dark. The same principle applies to spiritual warfare. God does not reveal His entire plan at once, and neither should you. Revelation is often progressive, given in pieces to preserve safety, obedience, and trust.

The spirit realm operates the same way.

When Daniel prayed and fasted, the answer was dispatched immediately, but spiritual resistance delayed it (Daniel 10). If Daniel had spoken too soon or stopped too early, he might have forfeited the revelation. There is a rhythm to revelation that requires spiritual intelligence to manage. What you know in the spirit must be protected until the time of its manifestation.

Silence is not inactivity. It is information management.

There is a common misconception that silence means passivity. In truth, spiritual silence is an active discipline. It is the management of information, the concealment of strategies, and the preservation of purpose. It is the intentional withholding of speech not out of fear, but out of understanding. In the realm of spiritual intelligence, silence is not empty; it is encrypted.

Application: Silence in Leadership, Ministry, and Conflict

The Offensive and Defensive Power of Strategic Silence. Silence is more than the absence of sound; it is a calculated act of restraint governed by both emotional and spiritual intelligence. It is a multifaceted tool that operates on two fronts: as a shield to preserve authority, revelation, and healing, and as a sword to outwit adversaries, maintain leverage, and protect sacred things. In the hands of a wise leader, silence becomes a fortress. In the life of a maturing believer, it becomes a teacher.

Strategic silence does not mean being mute.

You can be speaking and still not reveal anything. Words can be offered for diplomacy while the deeper matter remains unspoken. This level of silence is not evasive; it is intelligent. It is not rooted in fear but in understanding. To be spiritually mature is to know when to speak, what to speak, and when to remain silent, even while engaging in conversation.

Leadership: Silence Preserves Authority Great leadership is not defined by how much is said, but by what is wisely withheld. When Samuel was sent to anoint David, God gave him strategic instructions. The true purpose of his journey—to anoint a new king—was concealed from Saul. Instead, Samuel told him only what was publicly acceptable: he had come to offer a sacrifice (1 Samuel 16:2). That was not deception. It was divine discretion. If the full revelation had been disclosed prematurely, David's life could have been jeopardized, and Samuel's mission interrupted. Silence preserved the mandate.

Leaders often lose credibility when they speak under pressure instead of from purpose. Strategic silence allows for internal discernment before public engagement. It preserves influence and builds trust. When your words are few but full of weight, people lean in when you speak.

Ministry: Silence Guards Revelation Until Release In ministry, not every insight is for immediate distribution. Some revelations are time-locked, given to be carried before they are declared. Speaking too soon can diminish their potency, invite premature opposition, or confuse those who are not spiritually ready to receive.

This connects directly with the upcoming teaching in Chapter 7 on Revelation as a Weapon. Let this serve as a bridge. Silence is a womb for revelation. What you don't say now may become the saving truth for later. *Moses remained silent at pivotal points before Pharaoh. Jesus waited thirty years before speaking publicly. Paul held mysteries close to his chest, saying, "I was caught up to the third heaven... and heard things so astounding that they cannot be expressed in words"* (2 Corinthians 12:4, NLT).

Ministers must learn to steward revelation with spiritual maturity and emotional discipline. Silence is often the only way to protect what heaven has entrusted until its appointed time.

Relationships and Conflict: Silence Can Heal or Harm In relationships, silence is a double-edged sword. It can be healing when it creates space for reflection, processing, or recovery. But when weaponized, it becomes an instrument of emotional control. The goal of silence should never be punishment. Silence rooted in pride, fear, or resentment is not spiritual; it is destructive.

As previously noted in Misused Silence, punitive or manipulative silence is especially harmful to those who crave acceptance. It creates confusion, shame, and emotional instability. However, when governed by love and discernment, silence can de-escalate tension, prevent regret, and give room for divine healing to work.

Spiritually governed silence in relationships is about timing, tone, and motive. There are moments when words would only escalate pain, and seasons when God instructs us to step back and let Him speak. Discernment is what determines whether your silence is a bridge to healing or a barrier to connection.

Governed Silence, Not Emotional Silence Silence must be governed—not by mood, pressure, or fear—but by divine strategy. Emotional silence is reactive. Strategic silence is proactive. Silence that heals, protects, and preserves must be filtered through both emotional maturity and spiritual discernment.

This is not passivity; it is power. It is not weakness; it is wisdom. It is the kind of silence Jesus displayed before Pilate. He had every right to speak, but His silence fulfilled prophecy and preserved the divine agenda. That silence secured our salvation.

Silence is not absence. It is alignment. It aligns your soul with heaven's timing. It preserves your leadership edge. It guards the treasure of revelation. It heals where speech may harm. Those who master it will not only win wars but also walk in wisdom.

Mastering the Weapon of Silence Silence is one of the most overlooked weapons in the believer's arsenal. Yet when wielded with discernment, it becomes both sword and shield—offensive and defensive, subtle yet powerful.

It protects revelation, guarding divine secrets until their appointed time. It preserves stamina, allowing the soul to reset and the spirit to hear clearly. It prevents premature loss, keeping destiny intact by avoiding battles that words could escalate. Most importantly, silence invokes divine intervention—creating space for God to act when human speech would only interfere.

Jesus modeled it in His trial. He refused to defend Himself before Herod or Pilate, fulfilling prophecy and aligning with a higher purpose. Abigail leveraged it in her marriage and in crisis, choosing carefully when to speak and when to hold her peace until the right moment to act. In both cases, silence was not weakness; it was strategic brilliance.

When used rightly, silence gives you an unfair advantage in warfare. It blinds the enemy, preserves your footing, and amplifies your discernment. In a world full of noise, silence is a force multiplier.

Sometimes, the most powerful thing you can say... is nothing at all.

Chapter 6

Wisdom is a Weapon of War

"Wisdom is the principal thing; therefore get wisdom. And in all your getting, get understanding." —Proverbs 4:7

There are weapons that do not feel like weapons—tools so interwoven into our daily lives that we often reduce them to mere virtues, missing their true potency in battle. Wisdom and humility are two such weapons. Like giving and silence, they are multifunctional, operating both as offensive and defensive strategies. They are not reserved for altars or emergencies. They are used in boardrooms and prayer rooms, in conflicts and conversations, in correction and restraint.

But unlike more dramatic forms of warfare, wisdom and humility operate in subtlety. They do not shout, yet they speak. They do not wound, yet they win. To wield them properly, one must recognize that life's greatest battles are rarely fought with swords or missiles. They are fought in decisions, conversations, betrayals, pressures, delays, and power plays.

We begin with wisdom—the principal thing.

1. The Two Sides of Wisdom: Divine Wisdom vs. Diplomatic Intelligence Not all wisdom is divine. In fact, one of the enemy's greatest deceptions is to offer intelligence that mimics wisdom but is rooted in fear, pride, or self-preservation.

- Divine wisdom flows from reverence for God, governed by spiritual insight and eternal alignment.
- Diplomatic wisdom (or intelligence) is rooted in strategy without submission—it seeks peace at the cost of truth, often masking fear with finesse.

Diplomatic intelligence may preserve your image, but it can trap your destiny. It teaches you how to "play it safe" in rooms where truth must roar. It calculates survival but cancels assignment.

True wisdom, on the other hand, is both discerning and decisive. It sees through deception and speaks with timing. It does not trade integrity for access, or righteousness for relevance. It sacrifices comfort to preserve purpose.

Biblical Contrast: Solomon vs. Absalom

- Solomon demonstrated divine wisdom when he judged the two mothers contending over a child. His discernment uncovered truth without accusation.
- Absalom, David's son, employed diplomatic wisdom. He stood at the gate, flattering the people, positioning himself as more "understanding" than his father. That diplomacy gained followers—but it was a trap that ended in destruction.

Diplomacy seeks approval; divine wisdom seeks alignment with purpose.

The Four Types of Wisdom: Discerning the Voices that Guide

"Who among you is wise and understanding? Let him show it by his good life, by deeds done in the humility that comes from wisdom." —James 3:13, NIV

One of the most overlooked dimensions of warfare is the source of guidance we follow. We often assume wisdom is always noble, always divine, always safe. But Scripture warns otherwise. Not all wisdom comes from God. Some wisdom is cunning. Some wisdom is emotional. Some wisdom is outright demonic—packaged in insight but seeded in rebellion. And unless we learn to discern the source, we may find ourselves defending darkness in the name of brilliance.

The book of James unveils a critical classification of wisdom—one that is essential for navigating both spiritual warfare and the delicate terrains of leadership, ministry, and destiny. It outlines four types of wisdom, each with distinct origins, characteristics, and outcomes.

Let us walk through these not as mere categories, but as spiritual voices competing for our allegiance.

1. Earthly Wisdom: The Reasoning of the Natural Mind
Earthly wisdom is the most common form of wisdom. It is built through experience, observation, education, and social conditioning. It is the wisdom of logic, common sense, and worldly systems. It helps us manage life in the natural world—balancing budgets, negotiating relationships, or navigating cultural norms. It is neither evil nor inherently flawed, but it is limited.

This kind of wisdom is useful in everyday decisions, but it fails in spiritual warfare. It cannot discern the invisible. It cannot interpret divine timing. It sees through the lens of cause and effect, not revelation. And therein lies the danger: what works in logic may collapse in the spirit.

Many destinies have been delayed because someone applied practical wisdom where divine instruction was required.

"There is a way that seems right to a man, but its end is the way of death." —Proverbs 14:12

Earthly wisdom can keep you comfortable, but not always aligned.

2. Sensual Wisdom: When Emotions Replace Discernment The second type of wisdom is far more subtle.

Sensual wisdom arises not from experience or truth, but from feelings, instincts, and unprocessed emotions. It speaks loudly in seasons of pain, anger, insecurity, or pride. It masquerades as authenticity, but it is unstable. It makes decisions based on how things feel, not what God says.

When sensual wisdom governs a person, they are easily swayed by offense, fear, or flattery. They may call it discernment, but it is really projection. They don't just feel pain; they interpret every interaction through that pain. They don't just sense urgency; they confuse it for direction. And so they speak, act, and decide—not from the Spirit, but from the soul.

Sensual wisdom thrives in unhealed wounds.

This wisdom cannot be acquired; it must be unlearned. It is not a tool to embrace, but a distortion to crucify.

3. Demonic Wisdom: The Intelligence of Darkness This may be the most alarming type of wisdom—because it is intelligent, strategic, and effective, yet completely opposed to the will of God. James describes this wisdom as "earthly, sensual, demonic," and warns that it produces envy, strife, confusion, and every evil work (James 3:15–16).

Demonic wisdom knows how to build empires, manipulate emotions, hijack loyalty, and mask pride in religious language. It is the wisdom of rebellion—the insight of serpents. In today's language, it is what fuels spiritual narcissism, religious control, political deception, and strategic betrayal. It is cunning, not wise. It is clever, not pure.

Unlike sensual wisdom, which arises from within, demonic wisdom is imparted—often through association, compromise, or generational systems of pride. It is what Satan offered Eve in Eden: "You shall be as gods." The tragedy? She desired the wisdom of darkness while already clothed in the glory of light.

You don't need to study demonic wisdom to resist it. You only need to walk in the purity and discernment of God's wisdom, which exposes every counterfeit by its fruit.

4. Divine Wisdom: The Intelligence of Heaven (Expanded with Scripture) Divine wisdom is unlike any other kind. It flows from above, unmarred by human motives or emotional instability. It is pure, peaceable, gentle, full of mercy and good fruit, impartial and sincere (James 3:17). It is the wisdom that sees through time, reveals the heart, and aligns you with divine timing and eternal outcomes.

This wisdom does not merely help you survive battles; it helps you win them without unnecessary scars. It is what preserved Esther's timing, Joseph's perspective, and Jesus' silence. Divine wisdom doesn't operate through volume, vengeance, or visibility—it flows through alignment and insight.

And perhaps the most startling truth is this: Even what appears foolish in the eyes of man is wiser than the most brilliant strategies of earth.

"Because the foolishness of God is wiser than men, and the weakness of God is stronger than men." —1 Corinthians 1:25

This verse is not just poetic—it is deeply theological. It reminds us that God's wisdom often looks illogical when viewed through the lens of human rationale. But that is precisely what makes it powerful. The Cross looked foolish. Silence before Pilate seemed weak. Choosing a teenage girl to birth the Messiah was unthinkable. Yet in all these, God's wisdom prevailed and confounded the wise.

Divine wisdom is not just higher—it is wholly other. It cannot be reasoned into. It must be received.

"If any of you lacks wisdom, let him ask of God, who gives to all liberally and without reproach, and it will be given to him." —James 1:5

When we engage divine wisdom in warfare, we step into the mind of Christ, not just the strategies of men. It turns battles into breakthroughs and makes defeat impossible—even when it looks delayed.

A Word to the Warrior You will face moments when every type of wisdom seems reasonable.

- Earthly wisdom will appeal to logic.
- Sensual wisdom will echo your feelings.
- Demonic wisdom will promise quick results.
- But only divine wisdom will preserve your soul.

This is why James warns us to "ask for wisdom"—not just possess it. Wisdom must be received from above, not pulled from within. It is not just a tool; it is a dimension of God Himself. And to walk in divine wisdom is to walk in alignment with the mind of God in every decision.

So the question in warfare is not, "What is the smart move?" The question is, "Whose wisdom am I using?"

Wisdom's House and Her Hidden Treasures: The Structural and Spiritual Power of Divine Intelligence

"Wisdom has built her house; she has hewn out her seven pillars." —Proverbs 9:1

"The foolishness of God is wiser than the wisdom of men." —1 Corinthians 1:25

The Architecture of Wisdom Wisdom is not merely a trait to be admired—it is a dwelling to be inhabited. When the Scripture declares that "Wisdom has built her house," it is unveiling a spiritual blueprint. This is not metaphor alone. This is the Spirit of God revealing how life—strong, stable, and secure life—is to be constructed.

Wisdom is a builder. She works with eternal material. Her foundations are unshakable, her pillars immovable. And yet, many treat wisdom as an optional upgrade, not the structural framework of victorious living. But wisdom does not decorate foolishness. She builds where there is alignment. She strengthens those who walk in obedience. Her house is not a concept—it is a place of power.

But what holds up this house? What gives wisdom its strength?

The Seven Pillars of Wisdom (James 3:17) While Proverbs 9 introduces the concept of wisdom's seven pillars, James 3:17 gives us a vivid picture of what they look like in practice. These are the inner columns that support her house—divine traits that make wisdom weight-bearing and warfare-ready:

1. Purity – The Foundation of All Wisdom True wisdom begins with purity—of heart, motive, and intent. This pillar ensures that your decisions are not polluted by envy, ambition, or manipulation. Purity aligns wisdom with God's heart.

Where there is compromise, wisdom becomes corrupted. Purity is the guardrail that keeps wisdom from becoming cunning.

How to acquire it: Purity is birthed in the fear of the Lord and maintained through consecration. It requires surrender, not just strategy.

2. Peaceability – Wisdom That Seeks Harmony, Not Chaos This doesn't mean peace at all costs. It means that wisdom always seeks the path of peace before the path of war. It evaluates what can be resolved without unnecessary bloodshed.

Peaceability protects your energy from avoidable conflict.

How to acquire it: Practice restraint. Study the art of de-escalation. Pray for discernment to know when peace is a weapon, not a weakness.

3. Gentleness – Power With Soft Edges Wisdom doesn't bulldoze its way through. It is strong but not harsh. Wisdom knows that authority is not proven by volume or force, but by confidence in truth.

Gentleness is not silence; it is strength wrapped in calm.

How to acquire it: Cultivate humility. Learn from leaders who were firm but kind. Ask God to season your speech with grace and your reactions with control.

4. Willingness to Yield – Flexibility Without Compromise This is the pillar that keeps wisdom from becoming stubborn. It's the ability to listen, adapt, and adjust without violating truth. Wisdom knows when to stand and when to yield.

This is not submission to error, but openness to better insight.

How to acquire it: Be teachable. Learn to take feedback. Submit your opinions to wise counsel. The unyielding are often the first to fall.

5. Mercy and Good Fruits – Compassion That Produces Action Wisdom is not cold calculation. It is rich with mercy. It considers not only what is right, but what is redemptive. Mercy makes wisdom life-giving, not just correct.

Mercy adds soul to strategy.

How to acquire it: Practice empathy. Ask, "How will this decision impact others?" Learn the balance between justice and grace.

6. Impartiality – The Ability to Judge Without Bias Wisdom must be free of favoritism. It operates in justice. Impartiality ensures that decisions are not swayed by personal gain or emotional attachment.

Where bias exists, wisdom is compromised.

How to acquire it: Anchor your decisions in principle, not personality. Ask God to remove hidden prejudice and self-interest from your heart.

7. Sincerity – Integrity Without Pretense Sincerity is the final pillar; it guards against hypocrisy. Wisdom without sincerity becomes manipulation. Wisdom that wears a mask cannot be trusted.

Sincerity ensures that wisdom reflects character, not charisma.

How to acquire it: Practice truth in your inward parts. Reject flattery. Speak with honesty, even when silence would be easier.

Wisdom is a System, Not Just a Spark These seven pillars reveal that wisdom is not a one-dimensional gift; it is a complete system of values and behaviors. Together, they form a house strong enough to handle storms, strategies, and seasons.

Wisdom without structure is like a sword without a handle. It will cut you before it helps you.

When we think of wisdom in spiritual warfare, we must no longer think of it as just a good idea. We must see it as a full tactical kit—with components, checks, and balances. It is not random brilliance. It is architectural intelligence.

These pillars are not passive. They are active reinforcements in the spirit. They shape how we lead, how we speak, how we make decisions, and how we war.

Wisdom's Co-Tenants: The Inner Treasures of Her House

Proverbs 8:12–14 (NLT)

The next layer of insight comes from Proverbs 8, where Wisdom speaks in the first person and unveils the spiritual companions she brings with her. These are not decorative virtues; they are divine instruments that reside within anyone who truly walks in wisdom.

Here is the full text of this powerful declaration:

"I, Wisdom, live together with good judgment. I know where to discover knowledge and discernment. All who fear the LORD will hate evil. Therefore, I hate pride and arrogance, corruption and perverse speech. Common sense and success belong to me. Insight and strength are mine." —Proverbs 8:12–14, NLT

From this passage, we see wisdom is not solitary. She is surrounded by—and in partnership with—key spiritual forces:

1. Good Judgment – This is the ability to perceive the consequences of actions before they manifest. It protects from unnecessary warfare.
2. Knowledge – Not the accumulation of facts, but the divine ability to know what others miss. Knowledge is spiritual advantage.
3. Discernment – The unseen radar that separates light from darkness, truth from deception, assignment from distraction.
4. Common Sense – Often undervalued, this wisdom is street-smart and situational. It knows when to be silent and when to speak.
5. Success (Sound Wisdom) – True wisdom doesn't end in theory. It produces strategic results in life, leadership, and spiritual warfare.
6. Insight – The capacity to interpret the deeper meaning behind events. Insight sees what is not said, what is not done, and what lies beneath the surface.

7. Strength – The ability to stand, to persist, and to endure. Wisdom is not just cerebral; it is muscular.

These are the co-tenants of wisdom's house. When you invite wisdom in, she does not come alone. She brings her network of power, discernment, and grace with her.

These companions of wisdom are not abstract ideas. They are tools of preservation, promotion, and protection. Together, they form a treasury of strategy for navigating relationships, leadership, ministry, and spiritual warfare.

Wisdom Is Not Just a Principle—It Is a Place To truly walk in wisdom is to dwell in a spiritual house that was built before the foundation of the world. In this house, you are not just protected; you are empowered. You are not just discerning; you are decisive. You don't just survive battles; you often win without lifting a sword.

Wisdom is a shield when attacked.

Wisdom is a ladder when trapped.

Wisdom is a lamp when darkness hides the way. Wisdom is a sword when deception must be cut down.

And when it seems like the foolishness of God—marching around a wall, raising a rod over water, speaking to dry bones—that is when wisdom is most potent. As Paul reminds us, "The foolishness of God is wiser than the wisdom of men."

Wisdom as a Weapon of Escape "Wisdom is better than weapons of war, but one sinner destroys much good." —Ecclesiastes 9:18

"For wisdom is a defense as money is a defense, but the excellence of knowledge is that wisdom gives life to those who have it." —Ecclesiastes 7:12

When Wisdom Becomes the Exit Strategy Not every victory comes by confrontation. Some come by outmaneuvering. And this is where wisdom reveals her quiet power—not just as a light for the path, but as an escape route in seasons of entrapment.

In warfare, both natural and spiritual, escape is not cowardice; it is survival. The presence of wisdom is often the difference between those who fall into every trap and those who walk out of battles untouched. Where brute strength may escalate conflict, wisdom diffuses it. Where speed may charge ahead blindly, wisdom sees the hidden snare and slows down. It is wisdom that says, “There is a time to speak and a time to be silent… a time to fight and a time to flee.”

Wisdom is not afraid of exit. It knows that premature confrontation can sabotage divine timing.

The Divine Role of Defense Ecclesiastes tells us that “wisdom is a defense.” In Hebrew, the word “defense” here also means a shadow, a shield, or protection—something that covers you from exposure. Just as money provides access and protection in earthly systems, wisdom functions as divine insulation in spiritual warfare. But unlike money, wisdom also gives life.

A shield doesn’t stop the war, but it absorbs the blow. Likewise, wisdom absorbs impact before it becomes damage. It detects what others overlook. It counsels your emotions before they overreact. It warns your spirit before you engage foolishly. When you are tempted to fight every battle that calls your name, wisdom holds your hand and says, “Not this one.”

Sometimes, escape is not about leaving the scene; it is about leaving the trap—emotionally, mentally, relationally, even spiritually. That is the warfare of wisdom: it allows you to stay in the battle while remaining untouched by its poison.

The Escape Blueprint in Action We see wisdom functioning as a weapon of escape throughout Scripture:

- Joseph escaped both Potiphar's wife and prison through strategic silence and divine timing.
- David escaped Saul—not once, not twice, but repeatedly—by discernment, agility, and God-given wisdom.
- Paul escaped assassination through knowledge of the city, alignment with allies, and Spirit-led timing.
- Jesus escaped premature death many times by withdrawing before "His hour had come."

None of these escapes were acts of weakness; they were masterstrokes of spiritual intelligence. Each move preserved destiny. Each withdrawal protected mandate.

As Ecclesiastes 9:18 reminds us, "Wisdom is better than weapons of war." This is not figurative; it is strategic truth. Wisdom can deflect an arrow you never knew was coming.

It can redirect a conversation, cancel a meeting, or delay a decision—all without confrontation, yet with massive consequences in the spirit realm.

Escaping the Trap Before It Closes One of wisdom's most powerful roles is helping you identify a trap before you need to fight your way out of it.

Whether it is:

- A conversation laced with manipulation,
- An invitation designed to lure you into emotional compromise,
- A battle you weren't called to fight,
- Or a decision meant to seduce your destiny out of alignment,

Wisdom sees it early. Wisdom sends red flags before the trap is even visible to others. It whispers, "Delay that reply." "Decline that meeting." "Don't defend yourself right now."

When you obey, you are not walking in fear; you are walking in divine intelligence. That is why wisdom is not just a weapon of knowledge. It is a tool of escape—a ladder out of the pit, a door through the fire, a shield in the line of fire.

Reflection: Let Wisdom Be Your Way Out Pause for a moment and reflect: How many times have you asked God for a breakthrough when what you needed was an exit?

How many battles escalated because silence was misread as weakness—and reaction was mistaken for wisdom?

Ask yourself:

- Where is wisdom offering me an escape today?
- Have I confused emotional strength with spiritual intelligence?
- Is my ego fighting a battle my destiny has no business attending?

There are victories that look like losses in the moment. There are exits that don't lead backward—but forward. Wisdom knows the difference.

The Spirit vs. The Gift of Wisdom Understanding Wisdom's Dual Expressions

"To one is given the word of wisdom through the Spirit..." —1 Corinthians 12:8

"The Spirit of the LORD shall rest upon Him—the Spirit of wisdom and understanding..." —Isaiah 11:2

Two Dimensions of a Sacred Force Wisdom is not a one-dimensional quality; it exists in distinct but complementary forms—the gift of wisdom and the Spirit of wisdom. Both are powerful. Both are from God. But they differ in how they operate, in duration, depth, and effect.

1. The Gift of Wisdom: Occasional Access, Strategic Moments The gift of wisdom, listed among the nine gifts of the Spirit in 1 Corinthians 12, is a supernatural download of divine strategy given for a moment, a decision, or a person. It is timely and transformative, but not constant.

This gift often comes upon a believer in response to a situation that demands divine insight beyond human intellect. It is powerful, but episodic. The person who receives it may still lack wisdom in other areas of life. It functions like rain; it pours when needed, but it doesn't dwell.

You can have the gift to instruct others wisely while still mismanaging your personal life. This explains why some highly gifted individuals still wrestle with repeated patterns of poor judgment. The gift works through you, but does not necessarily form you.

2. The Spirit of Wisdom: Daily Governance, Deep Formation The Spirit of wisdom, on the other hand, as found in Isaiah 11:2, is one of the seven Spirits of God. This is not a visitational gift; it is a resident Spirit. It governs how a person thinks, discerns, reacts, decides, and lives daily.

Those who walk in the Spirit of wisdom are not merely insightful; they are formed. Their temperament, posture, and priorities reflect a deeper knowing. Their wisdom is not reserved for public instruction; it guides their private decisions, alignments, and boundaries.

This is the wisdom Jesus walked in. He did not merely speak wise words; He lived as the Wisdom of God (1 Corinthians 1:24). Every silence, every parable, every confrontation, and every retreat was timed and shaped by divine intelligence. His life was governed, not just gifted.

3. A Biblical Illustration: Solomon's Rise and Decline To better understand this distinction, consider Solomon. God gifted him with exceptional wisdom, and his reign began with promise and brilliance. He judged wisely, built extravagantly, and governed powerfully.

Yet over time, Solomon drifted. He mastered external governance but failed in internal integrity. He amassed wives, aligned with foreign gods, and ended his life in contradiction to the wisdom he once displayed.

Why? Because he received the gift but did not nurture the governing spirit. He had the wisdom to judge others but not to discipline himself.

The wisdom that builds the palace may not sustain the soul unless it is rooted in a deeper spirit of governance.

4. Wisdom to Do vs. Wisdom to Be This distinction leads us to a crucial truth:

You can have wisdom to perform but not wisdom to become.

- Wisdom to solve problems but not to walk in discernment
- Wisdom to lead others but not lead yourself
- Wisdom for business but not for boundaries
- Wisdom in speech but not in silence

This is why some leaders burn out, some ministers fall, and some parents excel in public but are absent in private. The gift of wisdom helps you function, but the Spirit of wisdom teaches you how to flourish.

5. Wisdom Is a Person Jesus is not just wise; He is the Wisdom of God (1 Corinthians 1:24). Wisdom is not just a virtue or a strategy; it is a Person you host. When you walk with Christ, you gain access to a Spirit that governs every dimension of life.

As believers, our aim should not be occasional access but daily intimacy with this Spirit of wisdom. This intimacy transforms you from one who receives words into one who becomes a voice.

The journey from the gift to the governing spirit is not about performance; it is about pursuit. And Scripture makes it abundantly clear: wisdom is available to all who ask.

"If any of you lacks wisdom, let him ask of God, who gives to all liberally and without reproach, and it will be given to him." —James 1:5

This is a divine invitation. God is not withholding wisdom; He is waiting to be asked. The humility to acknowledge your need is the first step to receiving the spirit that governs wisely.

But wisdom is not just a tool or a virtue; it is a Person. Paul writes:

"Christ the power of God and the wisdom of God." —1 Corinthians 1:24

To walk with Christ is to walk with wisdom. To grow in intimacy with Him is to be transformed in discernment, speech, decisions, and strategy. Wisdom is not a distant force to summon; it is a companion to host.

Wisdom is not merely what you know. It is who you walk with.

Chapter 7

Humility is a Shield

The Posture That Preserves and Positions You for Victory

"Before destruction the heart of a man is haughty, and before honor is humility." —Proverbs 18:12

Humility as Heaven's Prerequisite In the economy of heaven, greatness is not measured by prominence but by posture. The path to true exaltation is paved not with ambition, but with humility. This is not merely a moral virtue; it is a spiritual shield, a positioning tool, and an access gate to divine help. Scripture is unambiguous on this matter: "God resists the proud, but gives grace to the humble" (James 4:6). Grace is the currency of divine assistance, and humility is the only posture that qualifies one to receive it.

Humility is not self-deprecation, nor is it the denial of your worth or calling. It is, rather, the recognition that all you have and all you are finds its source in God. It is the heart that bows, even when the hands are strong. It is the mind that yields, even when gifted with revelation. True humility is not performative; it is spiritual alignment. It places a person under the mighty hand of God, not as a gesture of religious showmanship, but as an act of intelligent warfare. "Humble yourselves under the mighty hand of God, that He may exalt you in due time" (1 Peter 5:6).

If pride blinds, humility reveals. It grants access to dimensions of grace that are not available on the mountain of self. Grace, the enabling power of God, rests upon the humble because the humble know where their help comes from. They do not demand glory; they reflect it. They do not grasp for thrones; they are invited to sit upon them.

In warfare—spiritual, relational, or internal—humility functions as armor. It disarms the enemy of his favorite weapon: pride. Satan cannot fully engage what he cannot provoke. A humble heart is not easily offended, is not quick to retaliate, and does not compete for recognition. These are the very traits that make humility a shield in the day of battle.

To be humble is to agree with heaven's ranking system, where the lowly are lifted, and the last become first. It is to surrender the illusion of control and to embrace the wisdom of divine timing. The humble wait well, listen well, and receive well. Without humility, no instruction can land, no correction can stick, and no promotion can last.

In every season, humility is the posture that God watches for. It is the prerequisite for divine entrustment. It determines how much you can carry without crumbling and how far you can go without being lost in the journey. The strength of humility is not in its silence or gentleness alone; it is in its deep roots, grounded in God, unshaken by applause or abandonment.

Humility does not shrink your value; it prepares your vessel.

Hidden for Preservation, Not Rejection *"It is the glory of God to conceal a matter; to search out a matter is the glory of kings."* —Proverbs 25:2 (NIV)

One of the most misinterpreted seasons in a believer's life is the season of divine hiding. It is easy to mistake heaven's strategy for man's rejection. Yet, in the wisdom of God, concealment is often protection. To be hidden is not to be abandoned; it is to be preserved. Humility makes peace with this truth.

God hides what He values. Like Moses tucked away in a basket, like David sent back to the sheepfold after a prophetic anointing, like Jesus growing in obscurity for thirty years—every vessel that will carry true weight must first survive the womb of obscurity. The proud despise this season. They view it as delay, as insult, as failure. But the humble discern it differently. They understand that what God is building is not just a moment; it is a man, a message, a movement.

Pride makes you allergic to anonymity. It demands to be seen, to be known, to be celebrated. But humility welcomes the shadows if that is where God chooses to work. Humility anchors your soul when visibility is denied and validation is delayed. It silences the need to perform and replaces it with the need to be formed.

To be hidden by God is not punishment; it is preservation from premature exposure. You may be ready in gifting but not in governance. You may have a voice but not yet the volume of grace to sustain what is coming. God hides you so you are not wounded by applause too soon or destroyed by scrutiny too early.

It is in the secret place that humility is tested. Will you still serve when no one sees? Will you still build when no one claps? Will you still obey when no platform affirms your labor? The answers to these questions reveal whether humility is your disguise or your identity.

The humble heart does not interpret silence as abandonment. It leans into it. It trusts the pace of God even when the hallway between prophecy and performance is long and silent. That trust is what shapes capacity. That posture is what draws heaven's favor.

When God hides you, He is not depriving you; He is preserving you for a time when your appearance will serve His agenda, not your ambition. Humility rests in that assurance. It doesn't rush divine timing. It doesn't demand a seat at the table. It waits until it is sent—not just ready, but released.

"He made His acts known to the children of Israel, but His ways to Moses." (Psalm 103:7)

The children of Israel sought performance. Moses pursued God's process. Humility is what separates the two. One demands results; the other submits to refinement.

If you are hidden, you are not forgotten. You are in God's safehouse, not His storage room.

Humility as a Weapon of War *"Clothe yourselves with humility toward one another, because 'God opposes the proud but shows favor to the humble.'"* —1 Peter 5:5, NIV

Humility is not a soft virtue; it is a spiritual weapon. In a realm where wars are often fought with words, pride, and posturing, humility offers a disarming force that neutralizes spiritual attacks before they escalate. It is defensive in nature, but deeply offensive to the kingdom of darkness because it removes the legal grounds of accusation and pride—Satan's primary weapon.

The Bible does not merely recommend humility; it commands us to clothe ourselves in it. Just as a soldier wears armor, the believer must intentionally wear humility to remain protected in battle. Without this spiritual covering, even the most anointed can fall prey to deception, arrogance, or offense.

Humility is power under control; it is not weakness, but a voluntary laying down of self-will under divine leadership.

What Humility Is Not

- It is not self-rejection or thinking less of yourself. That is insecurity, not humility.
- It is not timidity or fear of men. True humility is bold because it is rooted in God-dependence.
- It is not performance-based or rooted in cultural norms (e.g., bowing, kneeling) that lack heart alignment.
- It is not manipulation disguised as meekness to earn favor or pity.

What Humility Truly Is

- It is having an honest and accurate view of yourself—neither inflated by pride nor diminished by shame.
- It is God-centered dependence, where success is stewarded with reverence and failure is not identity-defining.
- It is the proof that you are safe to carry divine power. God will not entrust authority to a heart ruled by ego.

- It is the path to divine backing, as Scripture clearly states: “God gives grace to the humble.”
- It is how you know which battles are yours and which are God’s. The humble don’t fight to defend their name; they let God do it.

Humility, therefore, shields the heart from deception, guards the soul from entitlement, and ensures that the victories you win do not become the trap that destroys you. It is the armor against internal sabotage and the defense against spiritual pride.

The Hidden Warfare of Ego and Image "The greatest battles are often fought in silence—between how we are perceived and who we truly are." —Dr. Joke Solanke

There is a kind of warfare that doesn’t involve demons or curses, but is just as deadly. It is the warfare of ego and image; the internal pressure to appear right, strong, competent, or spiritual, even when we are not. This battle is deeply spiritual because it is rooted in pride, though it wears the cloak of confidence, sensitivity, or even humility.

Pride in Disguise: When Insecurity Is Not Innocent Many assume that pride only manifests as arrogance. But low self-esteem, image obsession, and over-sensitivity to how we are perceived can be forms of hidden pride. Why? Because pride is not always loud; it is simply an excessive focus on self, whether inflated or deflated. Insecurity says, "What will people think of me?" Humility says, "What does God think of me?"

When self becomes the center—whether through self-deprecation or self-exaltation—pride is ruling.

Pride is not just thinking too highly of yourself. It is thinking of yourself too much.

Saul: The Tragedy of a Prideful Insecurity Saul's downfall was not immediate rebellion; it began with an obsession with image. In 1 Samuel 15, after disobeying God's command, Saul begs Samuel not for forgiveness, but for public honor:

"I have sinned; yet honor me now, please, before the elders of my people and before Israel…" (1 Samuel 15:30)

This reveals that Saul feared reputation more than repentance. His anxiety about losing the people's respect outweighed his desire to obey God.

On the surface, Saul looked insecure and eager to please. But beneath that was a prideful heart that valued public validation over divine instruction. His need to look like a king became greater than his desire to be God's servant. That is the warfare of ego and image; it substitutes surrender with survival tactics.

Modern Manifestations: In the Workplace and Beyond

In professional and ministry settings, this kind of pride can lead to:

- Insubordination disguised as "I know better."
- Offense when corrected because ego has been wounded.
- Lack of favor due to an unteachable spirit.
- Strained relationships because of chronic defensiveness.

Many relational breakdowns, whether in marriages, teams, or churches, stem not from demonic interference but from the quiet warfare of ego. The inability to admit wrong, take feedback, or let go of offense is not a personality trait; it is a spiritual war being lost.

The one who must always look right rarely becomes right.

What we call “standing our ground” may be seen by others as arrogance, lack of teachability, or disrespect for leadership. Ego repels favor. And many people have lost strategic positions, promotions, or partnerships—not because of incompetence, but because they were unapproachable, combative, or overly sensitive.

A wounded ego fights imaginary wars, destroys real relationships, and invites unnecessary consequences.

The Image Trap: Trading Authenticity for Applause

One of the greatest temptations of leaders and believers alike is the desire to maintain an image rather than walk in truth. We polish our exteriors while neglecting our interiors. This is how hypocrisy is born; when image becomes more important than intimacy with God.

Jesus warned against this with the Pharisees. Their pride was not flamboyant; it was institutionalized in their religious image. They prayed to be seen, fasted to be admired, and tithed to be praised. Their spiritual ego made them incapable of receiving correction.

When we are more concerned with how we are seen than who we are becoming, we enter a war that only humility can win.

Reflection & Warfare Strategy

Ask yourself:

- Do I correct or cover up my mistakes?
- Am I more focused on appearances than alignment?
- Does feedback offend me or refine me?
- Am I secretly afraid of being overlooked or dishonored?

Each of these reveals whether humility is active or if ego is silently driving.

"The fall of many is not due to external battles but internal negotiations with pride."

Humility and Authority — The Shield for Power "Power without humility is like fire without containment; it will consume what it was meant to serve." —Dr. Joke Solanke

The battle for authority is often misunderstood. Many fight to gain visibility or control, but few understand that true authority flows through humility, not dominance. In the kingdom of God, the path to greatness is not up, but down. The lower you go, the higher you rise.

The Centurion: A Humble Revelation of Power In Luke 7:6–9, a Roman centurion sent word to Jesus to heal his servant. Though he had soldiers under him, he declared, "I am not worthy that you should enter under my roof. But say the word…"

Jesus marveled; not just at the centurion's faith, but at his understanding of authority through submission. The centurion's humility opened a portal of divine endorsement. He knew that being under authority granted him the right to exercise it. That is the divine technology of humility.

Submission is not weakness; it is strategic alignment with divine backing.

Moses: Meekness That Shook Nations Moses was described as "very meek, more than all people who were on the face of the earth" (Numbers 12:3). Yet, he wielded power unmatched in his generation—parting seas, commanding plagues, and speaking with God face to face.

His authority didn't come from charisma, eloquence, or strategic positioning. It flowed from a deep well of meekness; a humility that trusted God even when misunderstood by men. When challenged by Miriam and Aaron, Moses did not fight for himself. God fought for him. That is the warfare advantage of humility; it makes God your defender.

Meekness is not timidity; it is strength harnessed by surrender.

The Fallacy of Power Without Humility Without humility, power turns to poison. Leaders who lack internal submission often fall into manipulation, domination, or self-idolatry. This is not only true in ministry or politics; it happens in families, churches, and organizations.

The difference between authority that serves and authority that enslaves is humility. Pride seeks to be served; humility seeks to serve. Pride craves recognition; humility gives glory to God.

"God resists the proud, but gives grace to the humble." (James 4:6)

That “resistance” from God is a form of spiritual warfare. It means the heavens push back against your progress when humility is absent.

Humility as a Shield in Spiritual Warfare Humility is one of the most potent shields in warfare because:

- It disarms the enemy of accusation.
- It attracts divine help.
- It multiplies grace and favor.
- It produces endurance, which is vital for lasting influence.

Satan is not intimidated by your position, but by your posture.

He fell because of pride and is attracted to it in others. But humility causes him to retreat because he cannot operate in atmospheres where self has died.

Practical Application: Are You Wearing the Shield?

- When corrected, do you defend or reflect?
- When overlooked, do you pout or stay faithful?

- When promoted, do you serve more or demand more?
- When misunderstood, do you retaliate or stay silent?

These are not personality traits; they are tactical responses that reveal who holds the power: you or God.

The Paradox of Power In God's kingdom, the lower you go, the higher your authority. The more you surrender, the more Heaven backs your voice. That is why Jesus—the most powerful being in history—humbled Himself to the point of death and was therefore given a name above every name (Philippians 2:8–9).

"He must increase, but I must decrease." —John the Baptist (John 3:30)

This is not poetic language; it is a warfare strategy.

Signs of True Humility vs. False Humility "True humility is not thinking less of yourself; it is thinking of yourself less." —C.S. Lewis

In the realm of spiritual warfare and leadership, humility is not optional; it is strategic. Yet, not all humility is genuine. Some cloak pride in modest words, while others pretend weakness to avoid responsibility. Discerning between true and false humility is essential, especially when evaluating ourselves.

Internal vs. External Indicators Humility is first a posture of the heart, not just a tone of voice or choice of words. False humility craves recognition for appearing lowly, while true humility is content being unseen if Heaven is pleased.

- False Humility: Performs externally but harbors inner entitlement or resentment.
- True Humility: Surrenders internally and allows obedience to guide the outer expression.

What you do when no one sees you reveals who you are when everyone does.

1. Serving When No One is Watching The hallmark of true humility is silent servanthood. Jesus washed the disciples' feet in an upper room, not a public square. He chose servanthood over spectacle.

False humility serves when it is convenient, seen, or rewarded. True humility serves even when misunderstood—not for applause, but because it is part of the nature of Christ.

"Whoever desires to be great among you must be your servant." (Mark 10:43)

2. Receiving Correction with Joy Humility is teachable, not defensive. Proverbs 9:8 says, "Rebuke a wise man, and he will love you." Why? Because correction is a gift to the humble; it shows them what to improve without waiting for consequences.

False humility may nod in agreement while secretly offended or wounded. True humility thanks the messenger and applies the lesson.

Correction is a mirror; only the humble gaze long enough to change.

3. Not Needing Titles to Function Spiritual maturity shows in those who don't need positions to obey their purpose. Titles affirm roles, but they are not prerequisites for impact. Jesus didn't walk around demanding to be called Rabbi; He simply taught, healed, and served.

False humility hides from responsibility under the guise of unworthiness, but secretly craves titles. True humility steps forward without needing a label, and bows low when entrusted with one.

"A man's gift makes room for him..." (Proverbs 18:16)—not his title.

4. Preferring Others While Knowing Your Own Value
True humility is secure. It allows others to rise, shine, and lead, while resting in its own God-given identity. This is not inferiority; it is maturity. As Philippians 2:3 instructs, "In humility, consider others better than yourselves."

False humility devalues self in order to appear meek but often leads to self-sabotage or passive aggression. True humility esteems others without erasing itself.

Humility does not mean you think others are better than you. It means you are not obsessed with being better than them.

5. Not Exaggerating Weakness, but Submitting Strength
False humility often parades weakness to avoid expectation or responsibility. It sounds like: "Oh, I'm not good at that," even when capable, because the weight of excellence intimidates the ego.

But true humility recognizes strength and lays it down for God's use. Jesus knew He had all power, yet chose silence before Pilate. Paul knew his revelations, yet counted them loss for Christ.

"We have this treasure in jars of clay, to show that the surpassing power belongs to God..." (2 Corinthians 4:7)

This is not about pretending to be less; it is about offering your more on the altar.

Am I Operating in True or False Humility? Ask yourself:

- Do I get offended when unrecognized or corrected?
- Do I avoid visibility because of fear or false piety?
- Do I feel superior for being "humble"?
- Do I downplay gifts God gave me to seem lowly?
- Do I love to serve privately or resent it when unseen?

Humility is not self-hate; it is self-governance under God's authority.

In a world driven by self-promotion, humility is a weapon of spiritual resistance and relational peace. It silences the voice of pride, disarms the enemy, and positions us for promotion without striving. Humility doesn't shrink your light; it removes the smoke of ego so that the light can shine without distortion.

Authority and Submission in the Realm of Warfare The Rewards of Humility: What It Shields You For *"The fear of the Lord is the instruction of wisdom, and before honor is humility."* —Proverbs 15:33

The realm of spiritual warfare is governed by authority and alignment. Victory is not always about confrontation; it is often about positioning. In the kingdom of God, authority flows through submission, and submission is sustained by humility.

When humility is present, authority is reinforced. The humble are shielded from unnecessary battles, equipped for necessary ones, and positioned for rewards that only heaven can give. Let us examine five of these divine shields and rewards, backed by Scripture.

1. Humility Shields You for Honor *"The fear of the Lord is the instruction of wisdom, and before honor is humility."* —Proverbs 15:33

Honor is not something you grab; it is something God bestows. Many have reached for honor prematurely and found shame instead. Humility is the spiritual credential that qualifies you for honor without striving.

In leadership, ministry, or the workplace, when a person walks in humility, honor eventually finds them. It is not just a public reward; it is a spiritual endorsement. God honors those who honor Him—and one way to honor God is to remain humble even when exalted.

2. Humility Shields You for Promotion *"Humble yourselves, therefore, under the mighty hand of God, that He may exalt you in due time."* —1 Peter 5:6

Humility is the pathway to divine elevation. The difference between self-promotion and God-ordained promotion is sustainability. What you promote by pride, you must sustain by performance. But what God promotes through your humility, He also defends.

When you submit under God's timing and process, you will rise; but in due time. That delay is often protection. Humility ensures that you don't destroy your destiny by rushing your unveiling.

3. Humility Shields You with Access to Revelation *"The humble He guides in justice, and the humble He teaches His way."* —Psalm 25:9

Revelation is not just for the educated; it is for the yielded. God shares secrets with the humble, because they will not weaponize revelation to manipulate others or exalt themselves.

Prideful hearts often receive information without insight. But the humble receive insight, direction, and correction because they can be trusted to handle divine mysteries with discretion.

Revelation is withheld not because God is silent, but because He is selective.

4. Humility Shields You from Disgrace *"When pride comes, then comes disgrace, but with humility comes wisdom."* —Proverbs 11:2, NIV

Disgrace is not always about sin; sometimes, it is about refusing to bend when God is correcting. Pride hardens the heart and blinds the eyes. Disgrace often follows not because God seeks to shame, but because pride prevents course correction.

Humility is like a reset button; it allows you to return, repair, and realign. Many have been preserved from public downfall simply because they were quick to apologize, quick to listen, and quick to change. That is the defensive power of humility; it catches you before you fall.

5. Humility Shields You for Proximity to God *"I dwell in the high and holy place, and also with him who is of a contrite and humble spirit..."* —Isaiah 57:15

Humility draws God close. It is not about volume in prayer, but posture in spirit. The humble do not demand God's attention; they already have it.

God's presence dwells with those who are lowly in spirit, not because they are pitiful, but because they are safe for intimacy. Pride builds walls between God and man. Humility tears them down.

The ultimate reward of humility is not just victory in battle; it is companionship with God in the midst of it.

Humility is not weakness; it is wisdom wrapped in surrender. It shields you from premature exposure, unnecessary warfare, and spiritual blindness. It attracts what pride repels: grace, promotion, revelation, and honor.

Let it be said of us: that when God looked for people to lift, speak to, dwell with, and defend—He found us humble.

Chapter 8

Revelation Is a Weapon of War

Revelation Defined — The Intelligence Arm of the Spirit Realm

"The secret of the Lord is with those who fear Him..." — Psalm 25:14

This chapter is deeply personal to me.

People often ask how I survived some of the most unthinkable and destabilizing situations I've encountered in leadership, ministry, and life. The answer never fits neatly into a single sentence or strategy. That is because much of my preservation has not come by protocol, but by revelation. I have profusely benefited from the intelligence of God, communicated to me through diverse means at critical junctions.

As a leader, I have experienced divine insight in ways that still leave me in awe. There were times I knew a staff member would resign before they ever turned in a letter. On multiple occasions, life-altering crises were revealed to me ahead of time, allowing space for mental, spiritual, and strategic adjustment. Like the serenity prayer suggests, I've been given grace to accept what I cannot change—but it was often revelation that told me what to accept, what to confront, and when to walk away.

This is why I say with urgency: If you are a child of God and cannot hear His voice—at the very least through His written Word—you are at a disadvantage and shortchanging yourself in warfare.

What Is Revelation? Revelation is divinely disclosed intelligence—classified information from the Spirit realm that natural senses cannot access. It is the unveiling of what is hidden, the knowing beyond knowing, the light behind the curtain. While information comes through education, and suspicion through observation, revelation comes through divine connection.

"The secret things belong to the Lord our God, but those things which are revealed belong to us and to our children forever..." —Deuteronomy 29:29

In the natural, intelligence agencies like the CIA or Mossad are tasked with gathering classified data to preempt enemy action and protect national interests. In the kingdom of God, revelation functions as divine intelligence, allowing the believer to plan, preserve, and prevail.

Revelation Is Not...

- Not suspicion: Suspicion is rooted in fear or pattern recognition; revelation flows from divine insight.
- Not deduction: Human logic is limited to past patterns; revelation can bypass history to reveal destiny.
- Not information: What is available on the surface is not always sufficient for spiritual direction.

Why Revelation Matters in Warfare In warfare—whether spiritual, relational, personal, or organizational—revelation is a weapon. It allows you to see behind the scenes and act with spiritual intelligence. You don't just respond; you pre-position yourself. You don't just survive; you outmaneuver.

The devil trades in deception. God empowers us through revelation.

"In times of battle, a whisper from heaven can outweigh a thousand shouts from men."

Revelation vs. Information — Access Requires Maturity

"It is the glory of God to conceal a matter, but the glory of kings is to search out a matter." —Proverbs 25:2

In a world where information is everywhere, revelation remains rare. We live in the information age—an era that rewards those who know how to search, research, and compile. But when it comes to spiritual warfare, information is not enough. What you know may keep you informed, but what God reveals will keep you alive.

Revelation and information are not the same. Information is surface-level; it is what you see, hear, read, or deduce. Revelation, on the other hand, is what God discloses to you because He can trust you with what others cannot handle.

The Distinction: Logic vs. Light

- Logic analyzes patterns. Revelation pierces darkness.

- Information informs decisions. Revelation transforms outcomes.
- Suspicion reacts to behavior. Revelation reveals intent.
- Prophecy can quote Scripture. Revelation unveils divine strategy.

Anyone can memorize "You shall be the head and not the tail." That is Scripture. But revelation is what tells you how, when, and where to become the head—and what to sacrifice to get there.

"Revelation is not about having a prophetic gift. It is about divine trust and spiritual maturity."

Why Not Everyone Has Access In the realm of warfare, not everyone has clearance. Even in government, not every employee has access to the same intelligence—access is granted based on rank, reliability, and relevance. In the spirit, God operates the same way.

Access to revelation requires:

- Rank: How yielded are you to divine authority?
- Maturity: Can you steward what God shows you without reacting immaturely?

- Alignment: Are your motives pure, or would revelation become a weapon in your flesh?

Many seek prophetic insight but cannot handle divine instruction. Some mishandle revelation, using it to manipulate, gossip, or control. But revelation is not entertainment—it is divine equipment.

The Danger of Revelation Without Maturity When revelation comes to an unready vessel, it can cause more harm than good.

- Revelation without wisdom leads to pride.
- Partial revelation acted upon prematurely can destroy relationships or destiny.
- Divine intelligence shared in the wrong setting invites spiritual warfare you are not equipped to win.

God does not reveal secrets to impress you. He reveals them to prepare, preserve, or protect. That is why discernment and discretion are as vital as the revelation itself.

Kingdom Intelligence Is Not for Show Just like intelligence agencies do not publish classified data, God does not showcase secrets for public applause. Revelation is not about making you look spiritual—it is about making you function effectively in spiritual warfare.

- Joseph didn't boast about Pharaoh's dream interpretation; he gave credit to God and used the revelation to preserve a nation.
- Elisha didn't use his insight to intimidate the king of Israel but to protect his people from Syrian ambushes.
- Jesus did not always explain His movements. Sometimes He hid in plain sight because revelation told Him when not to show up.

"Revelation does not always give you answers; sometimes it gives you instructions. Obedience completes the puzzle."

The Danger of Misusing Revelation. Revelation is power—but power without discipline becomes liability. One of the most dangerous things a person can possess is partial revelation combined with full confidence. Revelation must be handled with maturity, restraint, and timing, or it can become the very instrument of defeat it was meant to prevent.

Not every revelation is meant to be acted upon immediately. Not every insight is meant to be spoken aloud. And not every divine disclosure is complete at the moment it is received.

Some battles are not lost because revelation was absent—but because it was misused.

Some battles require silence until revelation is complete.

Premature Action: Saul and the Cost of Impatience

Saul's downfall did not begin with rebellion; it began with impatience under pressure. In 1 Samuel 13, Saul found himself in a military crisis. The enemy was advancing. The people were scattering. Samuel, the prophet, had not yet arrived.

Saul knew the ritual. He knew sacrifice preceded victory. He understood the principle—but not the order.

Instead of waiting for prophetic alignment, Saul acted on partial understanding. He offered the sacrifice himself, stepping outside divine instruction and spiritual jurisdiction. The moment Samuel arrived, the verdict was pronounced: "You have done foolishly… your kingdom shall not continue."

Saul's mistake was not ignorance—it was overreach.

He acted on what he knew while disregarding what he was not authorized to do.

Revelation without patience will always tempt you to force outcomes. And when outcomes are forced, authority is forfeited.

Corrupted Revelation: Balaam and the Price of Greed

Balaam is one of Scripture's clearest warnings that spiritual access does not equal spiritual integrity. Balaam heard God clearly. God spoke to him unmistakably. Yet revelation passed through a heart still governed by greed.

When Balak sought to manipulate divine power through payment, Balaam knew the truth—but desired the reward. Though God forbade him from cursing Israel, Balaam eventually found another way: he revealed strategy to Israel's enemies on how to corrupt them from within.

Balaam did not misuse revelation through haste—but through compromise.

Revelation filtered through an unsubmitted heart becomes transactional. It no longer serves God's purposes; it serves personal gain.

This is one of the gravest dangers of revelation: when insight is divorced from consecration, it becomes a weapon against righteousness.

The Peril of Speaking Too Soon Revelation is not only about what God shows you—it is about what He does not yet permit you to say.

Many destinies have been aborted not because revelation was false, but because it was exposed prematurely. Joseph's dreams were accurate—but his timing was immature. The result was betrayal, delay, and unnecessary suffering.

God often reveals in layers. Acting on the first layer as though it were the whole picture invites confusion and resistance.

Silence, in this context, is not fear—it is wisdom.

Silence protects revelation until the conditions for its execution are ready.

Why God Withholds Full Clarity God rarely gives full revelation at once—not because He is withholding, but because we are becoming. Maturity must grow to meet responsibility.

Revelation demands stewardship. It requires emotional discipline, spiritual authority, and moral alignment. Without these, insight becomes dangerous—not just to others, but to the one who carries it.

This is why Scripture repeatedly ties revelation to humility, fear of the Lord, and obedience. Revelation is not information to display—it is intelligence to deploy.

A Sobering Truth Revelation can elevate you—but it can also expose you.

It can preserve destiny—or accelerate judgment.

It can save nations—or destroy legacies.

The difference is not the revelation itself—but the character of the one entrusted with it.

To see is not enough. To hear is not enough. To know is not enough.

Revelation must be handled, not just received.

Revelation as Light in Darkness "The people who sat in darkness have seen a great light, And upon those who sat in the region and shadow of death, light has dawned." — Matthew 4:16

Revelation is not just illumination; it is rescue. When God sends light, it is not merely to expose but to preserve, instruct, and deliver. In the realm of warfare, divine intelligence becomes the lifeline that navigates us through the shadows of confusion, deception, and destruction. In a world clouded by the unknown, revelation is heaven's strategy to override darkness.

Revelation Preserves Lives Throughout Scripture, we see how timely revelation saved individuals, cities, and entire nations. God does not leave His people without insight; instead, He releases light when it is most needed—often as a shield in seasons of potential disaster.

- Abraham and Sodom: God revealed His plans to Abraham, not because Abraham asked, but because relationship births revelation. Abraham's access allowed him to intercede for Lot, preserving his nephew's life from the judgment of Sodom (Genesis 18:17–33).

- Noah and the Flood: Before destruction came upon the earth, Noah received divine intelligence to prepare an ark. What looked foolish to others became the lifeline of a generation. Revelation distinguished him as a man of faith and obedience in a corrupt world (Genesis 6:13–22).
- Joseph and Egypt: Through dreams and interpretation, Joseph discerned a coming famine and provided a national preservation plan. Revelation turned a prisoner into a prime minister. It wasn't just insight—it was economic strategy for survival (Genesis 41).
- Jesus and Herod: At birth and during ministry, divine intelligence preserved Jesus' life. Warnings in dreams kept His family away from Herod's murderous plot. Later, when enemies tried to trap Him in His words or accuse Him falsely, He answered with wisdom that confounded their plots (Matthew 2:13–15; Luke 20:20–26).

Revelation Delivers Nations and Destinies God's light is not for spectacle—it is for strategy. Every time light breaks into a dark season, it is a sign that God is actively preserving a destiny or redirecting history. Without revelation, many would stumble in decisions, relationships, and spiritual battles that were never meant to destroy them.

As Isaiah declared:

"For behold, the darkness shall cover the earth, And deep darkness the people; But the Lord will arise over you, And His glory will be seen upon you." —Isaiah 60:2

This is the power of divine intelligence—it creates visibility in obscurity, direction in chaos, and preservation in danger.

Revelation is not given for decoration; it is given for direction. In the day of battle, revelation is your map out of destruction.

The Failure of Emotion Without Revelation "For I bear them witness that they have a zeal for God, but not according to knowledge." —Romans 10:2

Emotion is real—but it is not reliable. In warfare, what you feel cannot dictate what you do. Without revelation, emotion becomes a weapon that backfires.

One of the clearest pictures of this is found at Ziklag, where David returned to find his city burned, his family captured, and his men weeping to the point of exhaustion. Even his own life was at risk as the people spoke of stoning him. Emotionally, it was a moment of total collapse. But instead of reacting out of grief or rage, David did something counterintuitive: he inquired of the Lord.

"David inquired of the Lord, saying, 'Shall I pursue this troop? Shall I overtake them?' And He answered him, 'Pursue, for you shall surely overtake them and without fail recover all.'" (1 Samuel 30:8)

This is the difference between emotional warfare and revelatory warfare. Left to emotion, David could have made a rash decision, risked more lives, or pursued the wrong enemy. But through revelation, he gained divine permission, direction, and guarantee of recovery.

Emotion without Revelation Leads to Waste Many believers weep, pray, fast, and war—but still lose. Why? Because zeal without revelation is like a car without a map. You may be moving, but you are misaligned.

Without revelation:

- We pray amiss.
- We waste energy on distractions.
- We engage battles God never sanctioned.

Revelation is what filters urgency from emotion. It separates what feels important from what truly is.

"Revelation tells you what to fight, when to fight, and when to be still."

There are times when the instruction is "pursue," and there are times when the instruction is "wait." You cannot discern the difference without the intelligence of the Spirit.

The Burden of Ignorance in Warfare Many have suffered needless losses—not because the enemy was stronger, but because they moved without knowledge. Warfare is not always won by intensity; it is won by accuracy.

God's desire is not just to give you strength to fight but to show you where and when to direct that strength. And that wisdom only comes through revelation.

Positioning for Revelation — The Posture of the Receiver *"Who may ascend into the hill of the Lord? Or who may* *stand in His holy place? He who has clean hands and a pure heart..."* —Psalm 24:3–4

"He reveals deep and secret things; He knows what is in the darkness, and light dwells with Him." —Daniel 2:22

Revelation is not merely a divine act—it is a relational exchange. And like all sacred exchanges, it requires proper posture. Heaven does not release secrets carelessly. Just as precious stones are not scattered on streets, divine intelligence is not given to the casual or indifferent. It is entrusted to those who are properly aligned—those who have cultivated the posture of a receiver.

Below are six essential postures that position a believer to receive revelation consistently and accurately.

Desire — Hunger Opens Portals God responds to hunger. The secret things of God are not uncovered by accident; they are revealed in response to desire.

"Blessed are those who hunger and thirst for righteousness, for they shall be filled." (Matthew 5:6)

Desire creates a spiritual pull. The deeper your desire, the more sensitive your spirit becomes. This hunger is not emotional hype but a yearning that lingers—asking, seeking, knocking until heaven responds.

Revelation doesn't come to the passive. It comes to the desperate.

Consecration — Clean Hands Attract Clarity Psalm 24 is clear: only those with clean hands and a pure heart ascend the hill of the Lord. The impure heart distorts divine perception. The contaminated vessel receives a mixture. But the consecrated one becomes a clear channel.

Consecration doesn't mean perfection—it means separation. It is a life set apart, cleansed from distractions, and purified in motive. God speaks to clean hearts because purity preserves the weight of the message.

Clarity in the spirit realm requires purity in the soul.

Stillness — Focus Filters Divine Frequencies In 1 Kings 19, Elijah encountered God not in the wind, earthquake, or fire—but in a still, small voice. Stillness is not just silence; it is focus. It is the elimination of internal noise so the whisper of God can be heard.

Stillness is a forgotten posture in a noisy world. But revelation requires internal quiet. You cannot decode divine intelligence when your spirit is restless and your soul is scattered.

Stillness sharpens spiritual perception.

Prayer — Engage the Revealer of Secrets God is the custodian of mysteries, and prayer is the protocol for access. In Daniel 2, when the king's dream threatened the lives of many, Daniel didn't guess—he prayed. And the mystery was revealed.

Revelation is relational. It flows in the place of communion. When you pray, you are not just requesting answers—you are engaging the One who holds the answers. This makes prayer a dialogue, not a monologue.

Revelation is not earned through works, but accessed through relationship.

Fasting — Heightens Spiritual Sensitivity Fasting weakens the flesh so the spirit can rise. It silences distractions, detoxes the soul, and sharpens perception. Jesus began His ministry after a fast—not because He lacked power, but to synchronize His spirit with heaven's agenda.

Fasting doesn't manipulate God; it aligns you with God. It prepares the vessel for divine deposits. Revelation requires capacity—and fasting creates space.

The thinner the flesh, the sharper the discernment.

The Vault Where Revelation is Verified God never reveals outside the boundary of His Word. Scripture is both the lens and litmus for any revelation received. All divine intelligence must be anchored in truth—or it becomes deception.

The Bible is not just a record of past revelations—it is a living vault. The more you dwell in it, the more you position yourself for fresh insight. The Holy Spirit brings to remembrance and unlocks layers of meaning only visible to those who dwell.

Scripture is not optional—it is the safeguard and foundation of revelation.

"Revelation is reserved for those whose posture proves they can be trusted with secrets."

Revelation and Divine Timing — A Shield of Preservation *"A prudent man foresees evil and hides* *himself, but the simple pass on and are punished." —* Proverbs 22:3

Revelation does not just show what to do—it often shows when. Divine timing is one of the most overlooked dimensions of revelation, yet it is crucial for preservation, favor, and results.

Jesus Himself declined premature exposure. In John 7, He told His brothers, "My time has not yet come," choosing to move in sync with divine timing rather than public pressure. Even Paul, as an apostle on assignment, was sensitive to the Spirit's timing—knowing when to go, when to wait, and when to pivot. In Acts 16, he was forbidden by the Holy Spirit to preach in Asia and instead was redirected to Macedonia. This wasn't a matter of logic—it was a matter of revelation.

Revelation without alignment to timing can become a source of danger. Knowing what to do but not when to do it has destroyed many divine assignments. David was anointed king long before he ascended the throne, yet he waited for God's time and refused to kill Saul even when he had the chance. Timing preserved his legacy.

Revelation as Preventive Preservation Sometimes, revelation doesn't instruct us to act—it warns us to pause, pivot, or prepare. It acts as a divine early-warning system, alerting us to hidden traps and instructing us on how to avoid loss.

Biblical Examples of Preventive Revelation

- Passover Instructions (Exodus 12): Before judgment came upon Egypt, God gave Moses specific instructions. The blood on the doorposts wasn't decorative—it was revelatory preservation. The death angel passed over homes that aligned with the revealed strategy.
- Noah's Ark (Genesis 6–7): Noah didn't build the ark in a storm. He built it by revelation, in advance. What others mocked was a divine strategy to preserve humanity.
- Elijah and the Drought (1 Kings 17): Elijah didn't declare drought because he was angry—he did it based on revelation. The declaration itself was a divine warfare tactic against idolatry, with specific timing and divine backing.

Revelation is God's pre-battle briefing. It preserves lives, destinies, and callings before the warfare even begins. It is the spiritual equivalent of being shown the ambush before stepping into the field.

Revelation in Everyday Warfare *"Men, I perceive that this voyage will end with disaster and much loss..."* (Acts 27:10)

"Do not be afraid... God has granted you all those who sail with you." (Acts 27:24)

Revelation is not a mystical luxury—it is a necessity for navigating the complexities of life, leadership, and destiny. God doesn't just reveal for ceremony; He reveals for survival, strategy, and success. In warfare—whether personal, professional, or spiritual—revelation is how we maintain advantage and alignment.

It is not always about knowing everything firsthand. Sometimes, survival is about being connected to someone who sees.

Joseph and Jesus: Revelation for Direction and Protection After the birth of Jesus, Joseph received a divine warning in a dream to take the child and flee to Egypt (Matthew 2:13). Later, he was instructed again through revelation to return because those who sought the child's life were dead (Matthew 2:19–20).

These revelatory instructions preserved the Redeemer and fulfilled prophecy: "Out of Egypt I called My Son."

Without revelation, Herod's massacre might have found its target.

This shows how even the Messiah's earthly life was preserved by the obedience of a man who could hear God clearly.

Revelation by Proximity: Elisha and the King of Samaria
In 2 Kings 6, the King of Syria planned multiple ambushes against Israel. Yet every time, Israel's army avoided the traps—because Elisha the prophet revealed the enemy's movements.

The king's frustration revealed a deeper truth:

"Will you not show me which of us is for the king of Israel?" (2 Kings 6:11)

But the answer was astonishing: "Elisha… tells the king of Israel the words that you speak in your bedroom."

You may not have the gift of revelation yourself, but proximity to those who do is a form of divine leverage. The king of Israel did not hear directly from God—but his connection to a man who did preserved an entire nation.

Paul on the Ship: Revelation in Crisis When Paul warned, “Men, I perceive...” his counsel was ignored. But even in the chaos of the storm, God’s voice reached him again:

"There will be no loss of life... only the ship."

Paul’s revelation didn’t calm the storm—it calibrated their response. That is the beauty of divine intelligence: it doesn’t always change the environment, but it empowers you to outlast and outmaneuver it.

Revelation Is Granted, Not Demanded Revelation is not a badge of spiritual accomplishment; it is a gift entrusted through intimacy. It cannot be claimed by merit, nor demanded through performance. Rather, it flows from alignment, proximity, and relationship with the One who knows all things.

In an age obsessed with performance and platforms, it is easy to confuse noise with depth. But God does not shout secrets in the open market. He shares them in quiet corners, with those who wait, listen, and love.

The Story of Two Sisters: Mary and Martha Few scenes in Scripture contrast posture and priority as clearly as the story of Mary and Martha (Luke 10:39–42). While Martha busied herself with serving, Mary sat at Jesus' feet, listening. The difference wasn't in effort—it was in alignment. Jesus called Mary's choice "the one thing needful." In other words, the highest priority.

Mary's positioning gave her access. Not because she worked harder, but because she valued the voice above the work. The reward was revelation.

The Secret Place and the Shadow Psalm 91 begins with this simple condition:

"He who dwells in the secret place of the Most High shall abide under the shadow of the Almighty."

The secret place is not a ritual—it is a realm. Those who dwell there don't visit God occasionally; they live in nearness. From that nearness flows an ecosystem of divine benefit: protection, perspective, preservation.

When Isaiah declared, "In returning and rest you shall be saved; in quietness and confidence shall be your strength" (Isaiah 30:15), he was highlighting a principle deeply countercultural: Strength in the spirit realm does not always come through activity. Often, it comes through rest. Through trust. Through quiet.

Proximity Precedes Insight Revelation is not unlocked by giftedness or spiritual striving—it is granted to friends of God. Psalm 25:14 says:

"The secret of the Lord is with those who fear Him, and He will show them His covenant."

This verse reveals a spiritual hierarchy. There are things God reveals to all, and there are things reserved for those who fear Him—who walk in awe, obedience, and friendship with Him.

God may give general guidance to the crowd, but He shares His secrets with those who are close. In the economy of the Spirit, proximity always precedes precision.

Why Revelation Can't Be Mass-Produced The hunger for knowledge in our digital age has not diminished—it has multiplied. But divine revelation cannot be reduced to formulas or replicated through spiritual algorithms. You cannot buy it. You cannot fake it. And you certainly cannot force it.

The greatest insights are whispered, not shouted.

They are reserved, not generalized.

They are birthed in the womb of stillness, not in the frenzy of spiritual activity.

This is why many powerful believers burn out while many quiet seekers burn bright. They know how to wait, how to listen, how to surrender.

PART III

Engaging the Enemy

Recognizing the true source of resistance is key to victory.

Chapter 9

When God Is the Opponent

There is only one opponent a person cannot afford to have.

Not Satan. Not people. Not circumstances.

God.

Every other battle carries an exit. Every other conflict allows recovery. Every other enemy can be outlasted, outmaneuvered, or overcome.

But when God becomes the opponent, there is no victory through effort, no escape through strategy, and no redemption without repentance.

Scripture does not present God as a casual adversary. It presents Him as the final authority. When He resists, the issue is not power but alignment.

"The Lord resists the proud, but gives grace to the humble" (James 4:6).

Resistance from God is not emotional. It is judicial.

Throughout Scripture, people survive demonic opposition. They survive human betrayal. Some even survive self-inflicted destruction. But no one survives sustained resistance from God.

David's life offers one of the clearest illustrations of this truth.

David fought battles on every front. He faced enemies without and enemies within. He endured betrayal, political instability, exile, and prolonged pursuit. He fought lions, giants, armies, and kings. He also fought internal wars of desire, failure, guilt, and grief.

At one point, Satan withstood David and provoked him to number Israel, an act that brought divine judgment upon the nation (1 Chronicles 21:1). The consequences were severe.

Lives were lost. David was broken. He wept openly and took responsibility for the devastation his decision caused.

Yet David recovered.

There were seasons when David was injured, scarred, depressed, and emotionally undone. There were moments when he cried until he had no strength left, when his men spoke of stoning him, and when his throne appeared permanently lost (1 Samuel 30:4). He lived as a fugitive. He was hunted. He was reduced.

Still, David always rose again.

The reason was not perfection. The reason was not strength. The reason was not privilege.

David never had God as his enemy.

God corrected David, sometimes severely, but He never opposed him as an adversary. Discipline did not turn into resistance. Judgment did not become rejection. Correction did not become abandonment.

That distinction preserved David's destiny.

Many people misinterpret suffering as proof of divine opposition. David's life dismantles that assumption. Pain does not mean God is against you. Loss does not automatically signal rejection. Warfare does not equal abandonment.

The real danger is not hardship. The real danger is misalignment.

When God is your opponent, effort is useless. When God resists you, spiritual language becomes noise. When God stands against a person, destiny stalls not because of Satan, but because of misalignment.

This chapter confronts the most uncomfortable warfare reality:

Some battles are unwinnable because they were never meant to be fought. They were meant to be surrendered.

Why God as an Opponent Is Absolute Defeat Not all opposition is equal.

Some resistance can be resisted. Some enemies can be fought. Some battles can be endured long enough to turn in your favor.

But God as an opponent represents absolute defeat, because this is not a battle of strength. It is a matter of authority.

When God opposes a person, He does not engage them on the battlefield. He removes the battlefield altogether.

Scripture is unambiguous on this point:

"The Lord resists the proud, but gives grace to the humble" (James 4:6).

The word resists does not imply irritation or emotional displeasure. It is a military and legal term. It means to stand against, to obstruct forward movement, to actively block progress. God does not merely withdraw support. He positions Himself in opposition.

This is why divine resistance is final. You cannot overpower the One who governs consequence. You cannot outrun the One who controls timing. You cannot outlast the One who authored endurance itself.

Satan fights illegally. Humans fight emotionally. Circumstances fight naturally.

God fights legislatively.

When Satan attacks, he must negotiate limits. When people oppose you, they operate within constraints. When circumstances resist you, they can shift with wisdom, time, or favor.

But when God resists a person, He writes resistance into the system.

This is why effort fails under divine opposition. Hard work cannot override divine order. Spiritual activity cannot cancel misalignment. Prayer without repentance becomes noise, because prayer is not a substitute for obedience.

Scripture repeatedly shows that divine resistance does not look dramatic at first. It often manifests as stalled progress, frustrated efforts, closed doors, and repeated failure despite increased labor. The harder the person pushes, the more immovable the resistance becomes.

This is not because God is cruel. It is because God is consistent.

God does not oppose people to destroy them. He opposes them because alignment governs access. When alignment is violated, access is revoked.

This is why battles against God are unwinnable. The person fighting believes they are engaged in warfare, but heaven has already ruled. The issue has moved from combat to correction.

Consider this sobering truth:

You can fight Satan and still win. You can fight people and still recover. You can even fight yourself and survive.

But you cannot fight God and remain intact.

Every recorded instance of sustained resistance against God ends the same way. Authority is stripped. Favor lifts. Destiny fragments. Influence diminishes. Not because God hates the person, but because rebellion is incompatible with divine partnership.

Many people confuse persistence with faith. Persistence is only faith when it is aligned with God's will. Otherwise, it becomes resistance disguised as devotion.

God does not negotiate with pride. He does not debate with rebellion. He does not reason with willful misalignment.

He resists.

This is why Scripture warns, not threatens. This is why wisdom teaches submission, not bravado. This is why the fear of the Lord is not terror, but intelligence.

To recognize when God is opposing you is not weakness. It is discernment. The wise do not ask how to fight God. They ask how to realign with Him.

Because when God steps into opposition, the battle is already decided.

David — A Man Who Fought Many Battles but Never God David's life dismantles the false assumption that hardship equals divine opposition. Few biblical figures endured as many sustained battles across as many fronts, yet few finished with such clarity of destiny intact.

David fought external enemies relentlessly. He faced wild beasts in obscurity, a giant in public, hostile armies in warfare, and a jealous king who hunted him like prey. Saul pursued him through caves and wildernesses, turning David into a fugitive despite his innocence. David lived displaced, misunderstood, and threatened for years.

He also fought internal battles. David's moral failures were public and devastating. His sin with Bathsheba fractured his household, corrupted his leadership environment, and introduced violence into his family line. His children mirrored the disorder he introduced. David carried guilt, grief, and regret that never fully left him.

David fought emotional wars as well. There were moments of deep discouragement when his strength collapsed under pressure. At Ziklag, after losing everything, Scripture records that David and his men "lifted up their voices and wept, until they had no more power to weep" (1 Samuel 30:4). He knew despair. He knew exhaustion. He knew what it meant to reach the end of emotional endurance.

David even faced spiritual opposition. Scripture explicitly states that "Satan stood up against Israel, and moved David to number Israel" (1 Chronicles 21:1). That decision brought judgment, national loss, and personal anguish. David was confronted by God, exposed by truth, and broken by consequence.

Yet David recovered.

He lost battles, but he did not lose destiny. He was corrected, but not rejected. He was disciplined, but not destroyed.

The difference was not that David avoided failure. The difference was that David never positioned himself in opposition to God.

When confronted with his sin, David did not justify himself. He did not blame others. He did not harden his heart. His response was immediate ownership: “I have sinned against the Lord” (2 Samuel 12:13). That sentence preserved his life, his throne, and his future.

David understood something many miss: God corrects those He is aligned with, but He resists those who refuse alignment.

There were seasons when David’s life looked like divine abandonment. He was hunted, reduced, stripped of stability, and pressed on every side. Yet Scripture repeatedly shows that even in those moments, God’s presence remained with him. Direction was available. Mercy was active. Restoration was possible.

That is not the profile of a man opposed by God.

A person opposed by God loses access. David never lost access. A person opposed by God loses correction. David was constantly corrected. A person opposed by God loses recovery. David always recovered.

Even when judgment came, God provided a way forward. Even when consequence followed, covenant remained intact. Even when David suffered loss, he was not cut off.

This distinction matters deeply.

David's life proves that pain is not proof of divine opposition. Struggle does not automatically mean God is against you. Tears do not indicate rejection. Discipline does not equal abandonment.

What destroys people is not battle. What destroys people is misalignment.

David endured enemies within, enemies without, and even spiritual assault. Some battles left scars. Some seasons left wounds. Some decisions left permanent consequences. Yet at the end of his life, David stood restored, honored, and aligned.

He finished well because he never crossed the line from correction into resistance.

David fought many battles. He lost some. He survived all.

Because the one opponent he never had was God.

Discipline Versus Opposition — Understanding the Difference One of the most damaging errors believers make in warfare is confusing divine discipline with divine opposition. This confusion has caused many to fight battles they were never meant to fight and resist corrections that were meant to preserve them.

Discipline and opposition are not the same. They do not carry the same intent, the same posture, or the same outcome.

Discipline is corrective. Opposition is resistive. Discipline keeps access open. Opposition shuts access down.

Scripture makes this distinction clear.

"For whom the Lord loves He chastens, and scourges every son whom He receives" (Hebrews 12:6).

Discipline is evidence of relationship. It assumes belonging. It operates within covenant. God disciplines those He calls sons, not strangers. Discipline hurts, but it does not reject. It wounds, but it does not sever.

Opposition, however, is different.

"But He gives more grace. Therefore He says: 'God resists the proud, but gives grace to the humble'" (James 4:6).

Here, God is not correcting a son. He is resisting a posture. Pride places a person in defiance of divine order. At that point, God does not instruct. He resists.

This distinction explains why two people can experience pain, loss, and delay, yet only one is being opposed by God.

Discipline says, "Return." Opposition says, "You cannot proceed."

Discipline includes instruction, warning, and redirection. Opposition removes momentum and frustrates progress until alignment is restored.

David understood this difference intuitively. When disciplined, he responded with repentance. When corrected, he yielded. This posture kept him within covenant, even when consequences followed.

Others did not make this distinction.

Saul interpreted correction as rejection and responded with defensiveness. Pharaoh interpreted discipline as inconvenience and hardened his heart. Balaam mistook divine restraint for interference and pushed forward anyway. Each time, resistance escalated because repentance never occurred.

Discipline invites humility. Opposition confronts pride.

Discipline operates in love. Opposition operates in justice.

Discipline shapes destiny. Opposition halts destiny.

This is why Scripture warns believers not to despise the chastening of the Lord. Discipline is not a sign that God is against you. It is often proof that He is still invested.

"My son, do not despise the chastening of the Lord, nor be discouraged when you are rebuked by Him" (Hebrews 12:5).

The danger arises when discipline is ignored, resisted, or repeatedly rejected. What begins as correction can eventually become resistance, not because God changes, but because the heart hardens.

A disciplined person still has access to:

- Instruction
- Conviction
- Mercy
- Restoration

A person being opposed by God experiences:

- Silence
- Stagnation
- Frustration
- Repeated obstruction

This is why discernment matters. Not every closed door is Satan. Not every hardship is warfare. Some struggles are divine interventions designed to stop a person from destroying themselves.

To mislabel discipline as opposition is to fight what is meant to heal you. To mislabel opposition as discipline is to endure what requires repentance.

Wisdom asks a better question.

Not, “Who is fighting me?” But, “What is God correcting in me?”

Those who answer that question honestly remain aligned. Those who refuse it eventually discover that resistance is far more painful than correction.

Discipline preserves destiny. Opposition protects divine order.

And knowing the difference can save a life.

What Causes God to Become an Opponent God does not become an opponent suddenly, emotionally, or without warning. Divine opposition is never impulsive. It is the final response to persistent misalignment. Scripture shows a consistent pattern: before God resists a person, He instructs, warns, restrains, and corrects.

When those measures are ignored, correction gives way to resistance.

The Bible reveals several postures that consistently provoke divine opposition. These are not isolated failures. They are sustained conditions of the heart.

1. Pride That Refuses Submission — King Saul Pride is not confidence. It is independence from God disguised as authority.

Saul's downfall did not begin with immorality or idolatry. It began with partial obedience justified by position. When commanded to destroy the Amalekites completely, Saul spared what God had forbidden and then defended his actions as strategic wisdom.

When confronted, Saul did not repent. He rationalized.

"Has the Lord as great delight in burnt offerings and sacrifices, as in obeying the voice of the Lord?" (1 Samuel 15:22).

Saul's pride was not loud rebellion. It was quiet defiance. He believed his role gave him the right to reinterpret instruction. At that moment, God stopped correcting and began resisting.

"The Lord has rejected you from being king" (1 Samuel 15:23).

This was not punishment for a mistake. It was divine opposition to a posture. Saul lost authority not because he failed once, but because he refused submission.

2. Persistent Disobedience — Pharaoh Pharaoh's story reveals how resistance escalates when correction is ignored.

God sent warnings before judgment. Signs before plagues. Opportunities to yield before consequences intensified. Each act of resistance hardened Pharaoh's heart further.

"The Lord hardened Pharaoh's heart" (Exodus 9:12).

This hardening was not arbitrary. It was the result of repeated refusal to respond to divine instruction. Pharaoh was not confused. He was defiant.

Disobedience became a pattern. Pride became policy. At that point, God did not negotiate. He opposed.

Pharaoh discovered too late that power without alignment invites judgment.

3. Resistance to Alignment — Jonah Jonah did not doubt God. He simply disagreed with Him.

When commanded to go to Nineveh, Jonah ran in the opposite direction. His resistance was ideological. He did not want mercy extended to people he despised.

Jonah's opposition to God's will triggered divine resistance. The storm was not satanic. It was corrective. The fish was not punishment. It was containment.

"You have cast me into the deep" (Jonah 2:3).

Jonah recognized the source. God was not fighting Jonah to destroy him. He was resisting Jonah's direction to realign him.

This story reveals a sobering truth: disagreement with God can place you in opposition, even when belief remains intact.

4. Spiritual Presumption — Balaam Balaam represents those who hear God clearly but attempt to manipulate outcomes.

God gave Balaam clear instruction. Balaam pretended to comply while searching for permission to do what God had already forbidden. His issue was not ignorance. It was presumption.

"Then God's anger was aroused because he went, and the Angel of the Lord took His stand in the way as an adversary against him" (Numbers 22:22).

Scripture explicitly calls God an adversary here. Balaam's spiritual gift did not protect him. His prophetic accuracy did not shield him. His refusal to accept restraint placed him in opposition.

Spiritual access does not replace obedience.

The Pattern Is Clear In every case:

- Instruction preceded opposition
- Warning preceded resistance
- Grace preceded judgment

God became an opponent only after alignment was rejected repeatedly.

This reveals a critical warfare truth:

God is never the first opponent. He becomes the final one.

Those who respond early to correction remain aligned. Those who persist in misalignment eventually discover that resistance is far more costly than surrender.

Divine opposition is not cruelty. It is containment.

And containment is often the last mercy before collapse.

Misdiagnosis — When People Think Satan Is the Enemy but God Is Resisting One of the most dangerous mistakes in warfare is not weakness. It is misdiagnosis.

Many believers assume that resistance automatically signals satanic opposition. When progress slows, doors close, or pressure increases, the instinct is to rebuke, fast, bind, and declare war. Spiritual language intensifies, but clarity diminishes.

Scripture warns that this assumption can be catastrophic.

There are battles you lose not because you are powerless, but because you are fighting the wrong opponent.

When God is resisting a person, Satan does not need to attack. The system itself works against them. Effort increases, but results diminish. Prayer becomes repetitive rather than revelatory. Movement continues, but traction disappears.

This is not demonic interference. It is divine obstruction.

"You ask and do not receive, because you ask amiss" (James 4:3).

James does not attribute unanswered prayer to Satan. He attributes it to misalignment. When the will is wrong, prayer becomes ineffective, not because God cannot answer, but because He will not authorize progress in the wrong direction.

This is where many people err. They escalate warfare language when heaven has already ruled.

Saul: Rebuking What Required Repentance Saul provides a sobering example of misdiagnosis.

After disobeying God's instruction, Saul continued to function in religious form. He offered sacrifices. He maintained appearances. He sought prophetic confirmation. But God had already withdrawn favor.

"The Spirit of the Lord departed from Saul" (1 Samuel 16:14).

Saul assumed his problem was external. He blamed David. He blamed enemies. He blamed circumstances. He never identified the real issue: God was no longer with him.

Instead of repentance, Saul pursued control. Instead of alignment, he pursued preservation of power. He even sought supernatural insight through forbidden means.

Saul fought everyone except the One resisting him.

Why Misdiagnosis Is So Dangerous When people misdiagnose divine resistance as satanic attack, they respond incorrectly.

They rebuke instead of repent. They fast instead of submit. They bind demons instead of surrendering pride. They look for deliverance when God is demanding alignment.

This error prolongs suffering.

"You cannot cast out what God sent to correct you."

Storms sent by Satan are resisted. Storms sent by God are yielded to.

Jonah understood this only after the storm intensified. He did not ask the sailors to rebuke the wind. He acknowledged the source.

"Pick me up and throw me into the sea... for I know that this great tempest is because of me" (Jonah 1:12).

Discernment shortened Jonah's suffering. Delay came from resistance, not the storm itself.

How to Recognize Divine Resistance Divine resistance carries specific markers:

- Increased effort with diminishing results
- Repeated closed doors despite persistence
- Loss of peace even when activity increases
- Silence where there was once clarity
- Correction without relief until surrender occurs

Satan attacks identity. People attack reputation. God resists direction.

When God resists, the question is never "Who is against me?" The question is "What am I misaligned with?"

The Humility Test The quickest way to identify divine resistance is to observe the heart's response.

Those under satanic attack cry out for strength. Those under divine correction are called to humility.

"God resists the proud, but gives grace to the humble" (James 4:6).

Grace returns the moment humility appears. Resistance lifts when alignment is restored.

This is why misdiagnosis is so costly. Pride prolongs opposition. Humility ends it.

The Only Weapon That Works — David's Secret When God is the opponent, there is only one weapon that works.

Not prayer volume. Not fasting length. Not spiritual vocabulary.

Alignment.

David understood this, not theoretically, but experientially. His wisdom did not come from distance. It came from proximity.

Before David ever wore the crown, he lived inside Saul's world.

He served in Saul's court. He married Saul's daughter. His closest friend was Saul's son.

David did not observe Saul from the outside. He watched him up close. He saw what the public never saw.

He knew Saul's decline was not political. It was not circumstantial. It was not demonic harassment alone.

Saul had lost the divine presence.

David knew this because he had become part of the system that tried to manage the consequences of that loss. Scripture tells us that David was brought in to play the harp whenever Saul was tormented, providing what we would today call emotional or music therapy so the king could function publicly (1 Samuel 16:23).

David watched the pattern.

When the music stopped, the torment returned. When the presence lifted, instability followed.

David saw something chilling: Saul was still king, but no longer carried God.

He was packaged well enough to appear functional, but inwardly he was deteriorating.

David understood something that many never learn until it is too late.

Titles survive without God. Crowns can remain without presence. Public function can continue even when divine approval has lifted.

David decided something in those years that would later save his life.

He would never repeat Saul's mistake.

This is the context behind David's most desperate prayer after his own catastrophic failure.

"Do not cast me away from Your presence, and do not take Your Holy Spirit from me" (Psalm 51:11).

This was not poetic language. It was intelligence.

David was not afraid of punishment. He was afraid of divine opposition. He was not bargaining for comfort. He was fighting for access.

David had seen what happens to a man who loses God but keeps position. He had lived inside the consequences of that reality. And when he failed, David made his priorities unmistakably clear.

Whatever discipline You choose, I will accept. Whatever correction You impose, I will endure. But do not remove Yourself from me.

Later, David expressed the same posture in another way:

"Let us fall into the hand of the Lord, for His mercies are great" (2 Samuel 24:14).

David understood that falling into God's hands was safer than standing against Him. Even judgment within God's hands was preferable to life outside His presence.

This is the secret that preserved David.

He knew God was not optional. He knew alignment was survival. He knew that opposition from God was irreversible.

That is why David could say, in essence:

Whom have I in heaven but You? There is nothing on earth I desire besides You.

He was saying, if You discipline me, I will take it. If you correct me, I will submit. Strip me if you must. Break me if you must. But do not leave me.

David made a vow in his heart long before he ever sinned:

I would rather be low with God than exalted without Him.

"I would rather be a doorkeeper in the house of my God than dwell in the tents of wickedness" (Psalm 84:10).

This was not humility rhetoric. It was strategy.

David was not perfect. He did not pretend to be. But he made one thing clear:

He hated what God hated. He refused to justify rebellion. He refused to normalize misalignment.

That posture ensured that even when discipline came, opposition never did.

This is the only weapon that works when God is the opponent:

Total surrender to alignment.

Not excuses. Not explanations. Not performance.

Alignment.

And the moment alignment is restored, resistance lifts.

The Mercy Hidden in Divine Opposition Divine opposition is often misunderstood because it feels severe. It interrupts momentum, dismantles plans, and exposes weakness. But Scripture reveals a truth that changes how resistance should be interpreted:

If God wanted to destroy you, He would withdraw quietly. Resistance means He is still engaged.

Opposition from God is not abandonment. It is containment.

When God resists a person, He is not reacting emotionally. He is protecting divine order and, in many cases, preserving the individual from self-destruction. Resistance is God's refusal to endorse a direction that will ultimately collapse the person He intends to keep.

This is why divine opposition often feels immovable. It is meant to stop forward motion until alignment is restored. God blocks paths not to punish ambition, but to prevent disaster.

David understood this mercy.

That is why he preferred falling into God's hands rather than being released to his own devices. He knew that unchecked freedom without God's presence was far more dangerous than discipline under God's authority.

Underneath God's resistance are everlasting arms.

Divine opposition says:

You are going too far. You are moving too fast. You are crossing a line you will not survive.

Correction still speaks. Conviction still functions. Grace still waits.

Opposition is mercy with boundaries.

This is why the most dangerous condition is not resistance, but silence. Silence means God has stepped back. Silence means the person is being allowed to continue without restraint. Silence means consequences will teach what correction could have prevented.

David never reached that point.

Even when he failed, heaven spoke. Even when he was judged, access remained. Even when discipline came, mercy framed it. That is why David finished strong.

The goal of divine opposition is never humiliation. It is realignment.

The moment alignment returns, resistance lifts. The moment humility appears, grace flows. The moment surrender occurs, access is restored.

This chapter is not a warning meant to produce fear. It is a compass meant to produce wisdom.

You can fight Satan and win. You can survive human opposition and recover. You can even confront your own failures and rise again.

But when God is the opponent, the wisest response is not warfare. It is surrender.

Because the safest place to be is not in control. It is in alignment.

And the greatest victory is in walking with God.

When Divine Opposition Turns into Divine Silence There is a stage more dangerous than divine opposition. It is divine silence.

Opposition means God is still intervening. Silence means God has stepped back.

When divine opposition turns into divine silence, Scripture presents it as judgment finalized.

Saul's life is the clearest warning.

After repeated disobedience, rationalization, and resistance, Saul reached a moment where correction stopped. Scripture records a chilling shift:

"The Lord did not answer him, either by dreams or by Urim or by the prophets" (1 Samuel 28:6).

God had spoken to Saul before. God had warned Saul repeatedly. God had corrected Saul patiently.

But Saul ignored every avenue of correction.

When God went silent, Saul did not repent. He panicked. And in that silence, Saul crossed a line he never would have crossed under correction. He sought guidance from forbidden sources. What discipline could have healed, silence exposed.

Silence did not mean Saul was free. It meant he was finished.

Scripture captures this principle in a devastating sentence:

"Ephraim is joined to idols, let him alone" (Hosea 4:17).

Those four words represent one of the most severe judgments in Scripture. Not destruction. Not rebuke. Not resistance.

Withdrawal.

When God says let him alone, He is no longer contending. He is no longer restraining. He is no longer intervening. The person is released to the full consequences of their chosen alignment.

This is why divine silence is more dangerous than divine opposition.

Opposition blocks progress. Silence removes protection.

Even in the New Testament, this principle holds.

Jesus warned Judas. He exposed his heart. He confronted his deception. But there came a moment when Jesus stopped standing in Judas's way. He did not restrain him. He did not intervene at the final moment.

"What you do, do quickly" (John 13:27).

That was not permission. It was release.

Jesus did not fight Judas. He let him go.

The final and most severe stage of becoming God's enemy is not when God resists you. It is when He no longer speaks to you at all.
No conviction.
No correction.
No restraint.

Silence.

This is why divine opposition is still mercy. Resistance still means engagement. Correction still means care.

Silence means the decision has been handed back to the person permanently.

David never reached that point.

That is why his cry was not, remove the consequences, but do not remove Your presence. He understood that silence was doom, but discipline was survivable.

This is the mercy hidden in divine opposition.

God resists so He does not have to withdraw. He blocks so He does not have to abandon. He confronts so He does not have to go silent.

The wise do not fear God's resistance. They fear His silence.

And they respond early.

Chapter 10

The Enemy Within

The Most Dangerous Enemy Lives Closest *"It is not the water around the ship that sinks it, but the water that gets inside."*

No battle can be won until this one is faced.

The most dangerous enemy is not the one confronting you openly. It is the one living closest to you. The one that speaks in your voice. The one that knows your history, remembers your wounds, and understands your patterns better than any external adversary ever could.

Many lives collapse not because of opposition without, but because of compromise within.

Scripture consistently reveals a sobering truth: external pressure only exposes what internal weakness permits. People often focus on what attacked them, who betrayed them, or what resisted them. But rarely do they pause long enough to examine what inside them responded.

What sinks a destiny is not pressure, opposition, or even warfare. It is what enters unnoticed, unchallenged, and unmanaged.

The enemy within does not arrive as an invader. It develops as a resident.

It grows quietly through:

- Unresolved wounds
- Unchecked thoughts
- Justified emotions
- Untreated trauma
- Compromised desires

This enemy does not need permission to destroy you. It already has access.

The danger of internal warfare is that it feels familiar. It does not announce itself as opposition. It presents itself as reason, survival, instinct, or self-protection. Because it feels natural, it is rarely confronted. Because it feels justified, it is often defended.

Yet Scripture warns, "Catch us the foxes, the little foxes that spoil the vines" (Song of Solomon 2:15).

Foxes do not destroy vineyards overnight. They ruin them quietly, over time. By the time the damage is visible, the roots have already been compromised.

Internal enemies work the same way.

No amount of prayer can compensate for an unexamined soul. No spiritual authority can override neglected wounds. No anointing can substitute for self-awareness.

This is why many lose battles they should have won. They fight externally while bleeding internally. They rebuke demons while ignoring dysfunction. They resist people while accommodating patterns that sabotage them from within.

Before Satan attacks, the enemy within often prepares the ground. Before people exploit, the enemy within creates vulnerability. Before destiny collapses, the enemy within erodes capacity.

This chapter does not accuse. It exposes.

Because no battle can be won without winning this one.

The war within determines the outcome of every war without.

The Three Domains of the Inner Enemy Internal warfare is rarely chaotic. It is structured. It operates within identifiable domains, each influencing the other, each capable of sabotaging destiny if left unchecked.

Scripture consistently presents the inner life as a threefold arena: the mind, the emotions, and the will. When these domains are aligned, a person is resilient. When they are fractured, the enemy within gains leverage.

1. The Mind — Where Narratives Are Formed The mind is the first battlefield.

This is where interpretations are made, memories are stored, and narratives are constructed. Long before a decision is acted out, it is rehearsed internally through thought.

"For as he thinks in his heart, so is he" (Proverbs 23:7).

The mind does not merely process information. It assigns meaning. When that meaning is distorted, behavior follows.

Internal enemies in the mind often appear as:

- Persistent negative self-talk
- Fear-based assumptions
- False conclusions drawn from past pain
- Lies that sound logical because they feel familiar

A wounded mind can interpret protection as rejection. A traumatized mind can interpret silence as abandonment. An insecure mind can interpret correction as attack.

These are not demonic attacks at first. They are unexamined narratives. And if left unchallenged, they become strongholds.

The danger is not having thoughts. The danger is believing every thought.

2. The Emotions — Where Pain Seeks Expression

Emotions are not the enemy. They are indicators. But when

emotions are allowed to lead instead of inform, they become weapons turned inward.

Unprocessed emotions do not disappear. They reposition.

Grief that is not healed becomes withdrawal. Anger that is not addressed becomes bitterness. Fear that is not confronted becomes control. Loneliness that is not acknowledged becomes unhealthy attachment.

Emotions demand expression. When they are denied healthy outlets, they find destructive ones.

Many internal battles intensify not because the person is weak, but because they have never been taught how to regulate emotional pain without suppressing it.

Suppression looks like strength. Regulation produces stability.

The enemy within thrives where emotions are either indulged without restraint or ignored without healing.

3. The Will — Where Direction Is Decided The will is the most powerful and the most dangerous domain.

It is possible to know truth in the mind, feel conviction in the emotions, and still choose resistance with the will.

The will governs direction.

This is why people can hear God clearly and still disobey. It is why insight does not automatically lead to transformation. The will decides whether alignment is embraced or rejected.

Internal enemies in the will often manifest as:

- Stubbornness disguised as strength
- Self-preservation elevated above obedience
- Control masked as responsibility
- Delay justified as wisdom

The will can override revelation.

This is why Scripture warns, "Today, if you will hear His voice, do not harden your hearts" (Hebrews 3:15).

A hardened will does not lack information. It lacks surrender.

How the Domains Work Together The danger increases when all three domains align incorrectly.

A distorted mind produces false conclusions. Unhealed emotions fuel reaction. A stubborn will locks direction in place.

At that point, the enemy within does not need Satan's assistance. The system sustains itself.

This is why internal warfare is so difficult to detect. It feels personal. It feels justified. It feels familiar.

But familiarity does not equal safety.

Victory in life requires mastery in these three domains. Not perfection. Mastery.

Because if the mind is renewed, emotions are regulated, and the will is yielded, external battles lose their power.

This is why the enemy within must be confronted before any other enemy can be properly engaged.

Biblical Portraits of the Enemy Within

Cain — When Desire Turns Hostile Cain's story is one of the clearest biblical revelations of how an ungoverned inner life can become lethal. Cain was not attacked. He was not tempted in secret. He was not ambushed by Satan. He was warned.

Before the act, before the bloodshed, before the irreversible consequence, God spoke plainly to Cain.

"If you do well, will you not be accepted? And if you do not do well, sin lies at the door. And its desire is for you, but you should rule over it" (Genesis 4:7).

This verse exposes the anatomy of internal warfare.

Sin was not attacking Cain. It was waiting. It was crouching, patient, restrained, dependent on Cain's response.

God identified the threat clearly. The danger was not external. It was internal desire that had turned hostile. Cain's offering was rejected, but Cain himself was not. Yet Cain internalized rejection as personal injustice. Instead of examining his heart, he nursed resentment.

This is where the enemy within took root.

Cain did not respond to correction with humility. He responded with offense. God gave him an opportunity to master what was rising inside him, but Cain chose not to.

Scripture says Cain became angry, and his countenance fell (Genesis 4:5). His inner posture changed before his actions ever did. The face revealed the heart. The heart determined the outcome.

Cain's greatest enemy was not Abel. It was comparison. It was wounded pride. It was ungoverned desire.

God did not confront Cain after the murder. He confronted him before. This detail matters. It reveals that internal battles are winnable when addressed early.

But Cain refused mastery.

Instead of ruling over his emotions, he let them rule him. Instead of confronting his jealousy, he fed it. Instead of correcting his offering, he targeted his brother.

The enemy within always seeks an outlet.

What is not healed internally will look for expression externally.

Cain's internal resentment eventually required a victim. Abel was not the problem. He was the projection.

This is why internal warfare is so dangerous. It convinces the person that someone else is the threat, when in reality the threat is unresolved desire and unexamined emotion.

Cain silenced the external voice that reminded him of what he was not willing to confront within.

After the act, God asked a question Cain could no longer answer honestly: “Where is Abel your brother?” (Genesis 4:9). Cain had lost more than a brother. He had lost alignment.

Internal rebellion had become external violence.

Cain’s tragedy was not anger. It was refusal to rule over it.

This is why internal mastery is not optional. It is survival.

Every person carries the potential for Cain’s error. The difference between mastery and murder is not exposure. It is response.

God’s warning to Cain still echoes today:

Sin may desire you, but you must rule over it.

Those who refuse internal governance eventually externalize destruction.

Saul — The Danger of Insecurity Saul's downfall did not begin with rebellion. It began with insecurity.

Saul was chosen by God, anointed publicly, affirmed by prophetic authority, and positioned as king. His problem was not lack of calling. It was lack of internal stability. Saul never resolved who he was before God, and that unresolved question became the enemy within.

Insecurity is dangerous because it does not feel sinful. It feels protective. It feels cautious. It feels reasonable.

But insecurity, when left unchecked, becomes a weapon that turns inward and outward at the same time.

At first, Saul's insecurity appeared mild. He hid among baggage when it was time to be presented as king. That moment was not humility. It was fear of exposure. Saul was already uncomfortable with visibility, responsibility, and comparison.

That discomfort never healed. It only adapted.

When David entered Saul's world, insecurity found an object. David did not attack Saul. David served him. David soothed him. David fought his battles. But insecurity does not require hostility to activate. It only requires comparison.

"When the women sang, 'Saul has slain his thousands, and David his ten thousands,' Saul eyed David from that day forward" (1 Samuel 18:7–9).

From that moment, Saul's internal enemy took control of his perception.

David became a threat, not because David reached for Saul's throne, but because Saul could not tolerate being eclipsed. Insecurity distorted reality. Loyalty looked like ambition. Competence looked like conspiracy.

This is how the enemy within operates.

It rewrites motives. It reinterprets facts. It assigns threat where none exists.

Saul's decisions were no longer guided by obedience, but by fear of replacement. His insecurity eroded his discernment. He began to protect position instead of presence, power instead of alignment.

As insecurity deepened, Saul's behavior escalated. He became suspicious, controlling, volatile, and violent. He threw spears. He chased David. He killed priests. He dismantled his own leadership structure in the name of self-preservation.

All of this happened while Saul still held the crown.

The enemy within does not need to remove position to destroy a person. It only needs to corrupt judgment.

Saul's greatest tragedy is that he externalized his internal battle. Instead of confronting fear, he pursued David. Instead of healing insecurity, he weaponized authority. Instead of repenting, he justified himself.

And as Saul's insecurity intensified, divine presence lifted.

What insecurity could not fix, control tried to manage. What fear could not heal, power tried to suppress.

This is the pattern of the enemy within.

It does not seek healing. It seeks dominance.

Saul did not lose his throne to David. He lost it to himself.

This is why internal warfare must be addressed early. The enemy within, when fed, will eventually demand sacrifices. Saul sacrificed relationships, integrity, spiritual clarity, and ultimately his destiny.

Insecurity is not harmless. It is lethal when left untreated.

And if it is not healed, it will always look for someone else to blame.

Solomon — Desire Without Restraint Solomon did not fall because he lacked wisdom. He fell because wisdom was no longer governing desire.

Solomon began with extraordinary clarity. He asked for wisdom, received it in abundance, and ruled with insight that drew nations to listen. His problem was not ignorance. It was appetite left unchecked. Over time, desire slowly displaced discernment.

Scripture does not record a sudden collapse. It records a gradual drift.

Solomon's heart did not turn in a moment. It tilted.

“King Solomon loved many foreign women… and his wives turned away his heart” (1 Kings 11:1–3).

Desire does not overthrow truth violently. It wears it down quietly. What begins as tolerance becomes accommodation. What is accommodated eventually governs.

Solomon knew the law. Solomon taught the law. Solomon wrote wisdom about restraint.

Yet knowledge did not restrain appetite.

This is the danger of the enemy within. It convinces the wise that they can manage what others cannot. It persuades the gifted that discernment exempts them from discipline. It whispers that experience can replace boundaries.

Solomon’s desire was not merely romantic. It was emotional, cultural, and political. He allowed intimacy to shape allegiance. Over time, what he loved influenced what he tolerated. What he tolerated altered what he worshiped.

“Solomon went after Ashtoreth… and Solomon did evil in the sight of the Lord” (1 Kings 11:5–6).

Notice the progression. Desire led to divided affection. Divided affection led to compromised worship. Compromised worship led to weakened authority.

The enemy within did not destroy Solomon's intellect. It redirected his loyalties.

This is why desire without restraint is so dangerous. It does not announce rebellion. It negotiates it. It does not deny truth. It delays obedience. It does not reject God outright. It shares Him.

But God does not share lordship.

Solomon's tragedy is not that he sinned. It is that he normalized compromise. The wisest man alive failed to apply wisdom to his own appetites. His inner life drifted while his outer life remained impressive.

Desire ungoverned eventually governs.

This is the quiet sabotage of the enemy within. It allows public success to continue while private allegiance erodes. It keeps the appearance of devotion while hollowing out conviction.

Solomon ended with words that sound like regret spoken too late: “Vanity of vanities, all is vanity” (Ecclesiastes 1:2).

Those words are not philosophical despair. They are the echo of a life that lost alignment internally long before it collapsed externally.

Solomon teaches a sobering lesson:

Wisdom does not replace discipline. Insight does not neutralize appetite. Calling does not cancel the need for restraint.

If desire is not governed, it will govern.

And when it does, even wisdom will bow.

Why Internal Battles Are Harder to Discern Internal battles are difficult to detect because they do not feel like warfare. They feel personal. They sound like your own thoughts. They move at the pace of emotion. They borrow the language of logic, self-protection, and survival.

This is what makes the enemy within so dangerous.

External enemies announce themselves. Internal enemies justify themselves.

Most people are alert to attacks that come from outside. They recognize hostility, opposition, and pressure. But when the conflict originates within, it is rarely questioned. It is assumed to be intuition, personality, temperament, or circumstance.

Internal battles disguise themselves as reason.

A fearful thought presents itself as caution. A wounded response presents itself as boundaries. A controlling impulse presents itself as responsibility. A resentful attitude presents itself as discernment.

Because these impulses arise from within, they feel trustworthy. They are rarely interrogated. And because they feel justified, they are defended.

This is why Scripture emphasizes self-examination. Not because people are inherently evil, but because the human heart is capable of self-deception.

“The heart is deceitful above all things, and desperately wicked; who can know it?” (Jeremiah 17:9).

This is not an accusation. It is a warning.

Internal conflict does not shout. It whispers. It does not push. It nudges. It does not demand. It suggests.

By the time the damage is visible, the decision has already been rehearsed internally many times.

Another reason internal battles are harder to discern is that they often develop slowly. External attacks create urgency. Internal erosion creates familiarity. Familiarity dulls discernment.

People adapt to internal dysfunction without realizing it.
They normalize emotional volatility.
They excuse relational withdrawal.
They rationalize chronic distrust.
They spiritualize avoidance.

What should provoke concern becomes routine.

The enemy within thrives in delay. It convinces people that there is time to address issues later, once life slows down, once pressure reduces, once circumstances improve. But unresolved internal conflict does not wait for convenience. It compounds.

Internal battles are also harder to discern because they often begin as responses to pain. Trauma, disappointment, betrayal, and loss shape internal defenses. These defenses may have once protected survival, but over time they outlive their usefulness.

What protected you once can imprison you later.

This is why people confuse coping mechanisms with character. Survival strategies become personality traits. Unhealed wounds become leadership styles. Emotional numbness becomes strength.

The enemy within hides behind past pain.

Finally, internal battles are harder to discern because they do not feel spiritual. They feel human. They involve emotions, habits, thought patterns, and reactions. Many believers assume that what is psychological does not require warfare. But Scripture does not separate the soul from the battlefield.

Internal warfare is not less spiritual because it is human. It is more dangerous because it is unexamined.

This is why many people lose battles they pray about but never confront. Prayer cannot replace introspection.

Revelation cannot override refusal to heal. Spiritual authority cannot compensate for emotional neglect.

Until the enemy within is identified, every external battle is compromised.

Victory does not begin with confrontation. It begins with discernment.

And discernment requires the courage to look inward.

How the Enemy Within Opens Doors for External Warfare External warfare rarely begins externally. It is invited.

The enemy within creates conditions that attract pressure from without. What Satan exploits and what people manipulate usually already exists as an internal vulnerability. External forces do not create the breach. They discover it.

This is why some people seem to experience repeated attacks from every direction. The issue is not constant opposition. It is consistent access.

Internal instability opens doors.
Unresolved fear invites intimidation.
Unhealed rejection invites manipulation.
Unmanaged desire invites temptation.
Unchecked insecurity invites rivalry.

Satan does not waste resources forcing doors that are already open.

Scripture reveals that temptation follows desire, not the other way around. Desire provides the landing ground. External pressure only accelerates what is already stirring inside.

People experience this as sudden warfare, but in reality, it is exposure.

What is not confronted internally becomes vulnerable externally.

This is why two people can face the same environment, the same pressure, and the same provocation, yet respond completely differently. One resists. The other collapses. The difference is not strength. It is internal condition.

The enemy within also signals to people what they can get away with.

A person carrying insecurity will attract controllers. A person carrying people-pleasing tendencies will attract manipulators.

A person carrying unresolved anger will attract constant conflict.

Human opposition often mirrors internal conflict.

This does not excuse abuse or exploitation. It explains patterns. Patterns persist until the internal condition changes.

Even spiritual warfare follows this principle.

Satan targets identity fractures, not wholeness. He attacks areas already weakened by neglect. He amplifies internal narratives that are already present. He suggests, but he cannot force. He plants ideas, but he cannot compel obedience without internal agreement.

The enemy within provides that agreement.

This is why Scripture emphasizes guarding the heart. Not because the world is safe, but because access matters.

A guarded heart limits entry.

A healed soul reduces vulnerability.

A regulated mind resists suggestion.

Internal alignment shrinks the battlefield.

When the enemy within is confronted, external warfare loses intensity. Attacks still occur, but they lack traction. Temptation loses appeal. Manipulation loses power. Conflict loses escalation.

This is not because the world has changed. It is because the door has closed.

Many believers focus on binding external forces while leaving internal doors open. That strategy is ineffective. Warfare language cannot compensate for internal neglect.

External victory is sustained by internal health.

Until the enemy within is addressed, external warfare will repeat. But once the inner battle is won, external enemies are forced to retreat or reveal themselves clearly.

The most strategic warfare decision a person can make is not how to fight others, but how to govern themselves.

Because when the enemy within loses access, external warfare loses advantage.

Weapons for Internal Warfare Every solution begins with accurate problem identification. Until we identify our unique internal tendencies, we will continue to struggle in denial.

Internal warfare cannot be defeated by denial, spiritual performance, or willpower alone. God has always provided resources for healing the inner life, and Scripture consistently validates them. These weapons are not optional accessories. They are divinely sanctioned tools for sustaining wholeness.

1. Truth — Renewal of the Mind Internal warfare begins in the mind, so God begins there.

"Do not be conformed to this world, but be transformed by the renewing of your mind" (Romans 12:2).

Renewal of the mind is not inspiration. It is intentional re-training of thought patterns. Scripture assumes the mind can be misaligned even in believers and must be renewed continually.

Biblical renewal involves:

- Examining thoughts (Psalm 139:23)
- Rejecting false narratives (2 Corinthians 10:5)

- Replacing lies with truth (John 8:32)

Application:

This looks like slowing down thoughts, questioning internal assumptions, journaling truth, and deliberately reframing experiences through Scripture rather than emotion. Without renewed thinking, emotional healing cannot be sustained.

2. Therapy and Wise Counsel — God's Design for Guided Healing Scripture never presents isolation as strength. It consistently presents wise counsel as a mechanism for preservation, stability, and healing.

"In the multitude of counselors there is safety" (Proverbs 11:14).

"Plans fail for lack of counsel, but with many advisers they succeed" (Proverbs 20:18).

Wise counsel in Scripture is not casual conversation. It is directed guidance applied to complex inner realities. What many now call therapy is the structured expression of this biblical principle: intentional counsel that helps a person process pain, regulate emotion, and regain clarity of judgment.

This concept is not modern. It is biblical.

Scriptural evidence includes:

- Saul and Music Therapy Saul's emotional torment required intervention beyond instruction. David's music stabilized Saul's emotional and mental state so he could function (1 Samuel 16:23).
- Job and Dialogical Processing Job's restoration did not begin with correction. It began with extended dialogue, emotional expression, lament, questioning, and processing. Only after this process did clarity and restoration follow (Job 38–42; 42:10).
- Jethro's Counsel to Moses Moses was emotionally and physically depleted under leadership pressure. God used counsel, not rebuke, to restructure his responsibilities and preserve his capacity (Exodus 18:17–24).

These examples reveal a consistent biblical pattern:

God heals the inner life through guided counsel before He restores function.

Application:

Therapy and wise counsel provide:

- Language for pain that prayer alone has not yet resolved
- Structured environments to examine internal conflict safely
- Tools for emotional regulation and self-awareness
- Insight that interrupts self-deception and unhealthy patterns

Therapy does not replace faith. It supports obedience.

Ignoring wounds does not make a person spiritual. Processing them with wisdom makes a person whole.

3. Emotional Regulation — Governing the Soul Scripture never instructs believers to deny emotions. It instructs them to govern them.

"He who rules his spirit is better than he who takes a city" (Proverbs 16:32).

David modeled emotional regulation repeatedly. He acknowledged sorrow, fear, and distress without allowing them to dictate his actions.

"Why are you cast down, O my soul? Hope in God" (Psalm 42:5).

David spoke to his emotions rather than being led by them.

Application:

This includes recognizing emotional triggers, pausing before reacting, naming emotions accurately, and choosing responses intentionally. Emotional regulation is spiritual discipline, not psychological weakness.

4. Boundaries — Biblical Protection of the Inner Life

Boundaries are not rejection. They are stewardship.

"Above all else, guard your heart, for everything you do flows from it" (Proverbs 4:23).

Jesus consistently practiced boundaries:

- He withdrew from crowds (Luke 5:16)
- He limited access (Mark 1:35–38)
- He said no without guilt (John 6:15)

Application:

Boundaries look like limiting exposure to harmful relationships, refusing emotional over-extension, and defining responsibility clearly. Healing cannot be sustained in environments that repeatedly reopen wounds.

5. Accountability — Exposure That Produces Freedom

Internal warfare thrives in secrecy. Scripture dismantles secrecy.

"Confess your faults to one another, and pray for one another, that you may be healed" (James 5:16).

Accountability is not control. It is visibility with safety.

David's failures escalated in isolation but were arrested when confronted. Healing followed truth exposure.

Application:

This involves trusted relationships where honesty is expected, patterns are addressed, and growth is monitored. Accountability stabilizes progress and prevents relapse into destructive cycles.

6. Spiritual Alignment — Integration of the Inner Life Healing without alignment becomes self-improvement. Alignment anchors healing in purpose.

"Search me, O God, and know my heart... lead me in the way everlasting" (Psalm 139:23–24).

Spiritual alignment ensures that restoration does not become self-centered. It keeps healing responsive to conviction, correction, and surrender.

Application:

This involves prayer, submission, sensitivity to God's voice, and willingness to adjust direction. Alignment ensures healing leads to obedience, not indulgence.

The Evidence Is Consistent Scripture does not separate spiritual life from emotional health. It integrates them.

Truth renews the mind. Counsel heals the soul. Emotional regulation restores authority. Boundaries protect progress. Accountability sustains integrity. Alignment preserves destiny.

These are not modern compromises. They are biblical provisions.

Internal warfare is won when the resources God has already provided are received, applied, and stewarded.

Because healing is not avoidance. It is obedience.

And once the enemy within is disarmed, external warfare loses its advantage.

The Governing Weapon: The Ministry of the Holy Spirit

No man can win the battle within sincerely without the help of the Holy Spirit.

Internal warfare is not merely psychological. It is spiritual at its core. The deepest conflicts of the soul are not resolved by insight alone, discipline alone, or even counsel alone. They require conviction, and conviction is not self-generated.

"When He has come, He will convict the world of sin, and of righteousness, and of judgment" (John 16:8).

Conviction is not condemnation. Conviction is illumination.

The Holy Spirit does what no human effort can do:

- He reveals truth without distortion
- He exposes sin without crushing hope
- He confronts the heart without destroying identity

This is why sincere internal victory is impossible without Him.

A person can manage behavior without the Holy Spirit. A person can modify habits without the Holy Spirit. A person can suppress symptoms without the Holy Spirit.

But transformation of the inner life requires conviction, and conviction belongs to the Spirit.

"The natural man does not receive the things of the Spirit of God... because they are spiritually discerned" (1 Corinthians 2:14).

Without the Holy Spirit:

- Truth feels optional
- Correction feels offensive
- Accountability feels intrusive
- Healing feels unnecessary

The enemy within thrives where conviction is resisted.

The Holy Spirit does not only reveal what is wrong. He also reveals what is misaligned. Much of internal warfare is not overt sin, but misplaced desire, distorted identity, and unhealthy attachment. These cannot be discerned accurately without spiritual illumination.

David understood this:

"Search me, O God, and know my heart; try me, and know my anxieties" (Psalm 139:23).

David did not trust his own perception of his inner life. He invited the Spirit to search him. That invitation is warfare.

The Holy Spirit also empowers what He reveals:

"For it is God who works in you both to will and to do for His good pleasure" (Philippians 2:13).

Conviction without empowerment leads to despair. Empowerment without conviction leads to pride.

The Holy Spirit provides both.

Without the Holy Spirit, these tools become techniques. With Him, they become instruments of transformation.

This is why Scripture calls Him the Helper.

Internal warfare is not won by striving harder. It is won by yielding deeper.

And the deepest victory is not achieved when a person conquers themselves, but when they allow the Spirit of God to govern them.

Because the battle within was never meant to be fought alone.

Chapter 11

When Opposition Has a Human Face

Why Human Warfare Is the Most Dangerous Kind

Human warfare is dangerous because it is unstable. Unlike spiritual warfare, where the enemy's nature is fixed, human conflict is fluid. People change. Motives shift. Loyalties realign. What looks like opposition today may dissolve tomorrow, and what feels like support can quietly turn into resistance.

There are no permanent enemies in human warfare. There are no permanent friends. There is only alignment—or misalignment—with purpose.

This is what makes fighting people so risky. You may be engaging someone who is not evil, not malicious, and not even hostile in intent, but simply not assigned to walk with you into your next phase. Treating misalignment as enmity creates unnecessary destruction.

Another danger of human warfare is emotional proximity. When the conflict involves people you once trusted, loved, mentored, or served alongside, the battle does not stay external. It becomes internal. Logic gives way to emotion. Discernment is clouded by history. Judgment is complicated by memory.

Spiritual warfare rarely feels personal. Human warfare almost always does.

This is why people conflicts exhaust the soul more than demonic opposition. When Satan resists you, there is clarity. When people oppose you, there is ambiguity. Motives are mixed. Stories are incomplete. Perspectives conflict. Truth becomes layered instead of obvious.

Human warfare is also dangerous because everyone involved is capable of growth, repentance, or further corruption. Today's antagonist may become tomorrow's ally. Today's ally may become tomorrow's liability. Escalating conflict too quickly can permanently damage relationships God intended to be temporary, transitional, or even redemptive.

Trying to be at peace with everyone creates another form of danger. You cannot be aligned with everyone and still remain faithful to your assignment. Friendship without discernment leads to compromise. Loyalty without boundaries leads to entanglement. Peace without truth leads to quiet erosion.

Some relationships are not meant to end in hostility, but they are meant to end.

Human warfare is therefore not just about opposition. It is about discernment of season, role, and assignment. Knowing who to confront, who to correct, who to distance from, and who to release requires wisdom that goes beyond emotion or principle.

This is why Scripture repeatedly warns against haste in judgment and reaction. Acting too quickly in human conflict often creates collateral damage that cannot be undone. Words spoken in anger linger. Decisions made in pain echo. Alignments broken publicly may never be restored privately.

Human warfare is dangerous because once it escalates, it rarely stays contained.

That is why this chapter does not begin with tactics, but with understanding. Before you fight, you must discern what kind of conflict you are actually in. Not every human challenge is a battle. Not every resistance is opposition. And not every opposition requires engagement.

Misreading the nature of the conflict is often more destructive than the conflict itself.

This is why strategy matters. This is why restraint matters. This is why discernment must come before action.

Because when opposition has a human face, the cost of being wrong is not just loss—it is lasting damage.

God as Father — Why Human Battles Are Rarely Clean

Human battles are rarely clean because God does not govern people as cases—He governs them as children.

God is not only Judge. He is Father. And He is the God of all flesh.

That distinction changes everything.

When conflict involves people, God does not respond the way we expect a courtroom to function. He does not always issue immediate verdicts. He does not always remove the offender. He does not always restore what was lost in the way we think justice should look.

This is not weakness. It is fatherhood.

A father does not destroy one child to prove another right. Even when one child is clearly wrong, correction is often measured, restrained, and timed. Discipline is applied with the future in view, not just the offense.

This is why human conflict often feels unresolved.

You may be right—and still unheard. You may be innocent—and still wounded. You may be faithful—and still overlooked.

God corrects, but He also preserves. He restrains judgment because He sees beyond the present moment. He sees trajectories, consequences, dependencies, and future intersections we cannot see.

As leaders, we glimpse this reality in small ways. There are moments when we recognize clear error, yet addressing it publicly would destabilize a system, damage innocent people, or jeopardize outcomes we are responsible to protect. So correction is delayed, quiet, or partial—not because the error is acceptable, but because timing matters.

God operates with that same weight—but on a divine scale.

This is why human warfare is emotionally exhausting. We expect God to act as an arbiter. He often acts as a parent. Justice is real, but it is rarely immediate. Correction happens, but it may not satisfy the wounded. Mercy is extended, even when it feels undeserved.

That tension is deeply uncomfortable—especially for those who have suffered betrayal, abuse, manipulation, or injustice.

Human warfare exposes a painful truth:

God may correct the offender without restoring the victim fully in the moment.

This does not mean God ignores pain. It means He addresses pain differently than punishment.

The danger in human warfare is assuming that because God does not act swiftly, He does not act at all. Or worse, interpreting delay as approval. Both assumptions distort God's nature and push people into bitterness, retaliation, or despair.

God's restraint is not endorsement. God's mercy is not blindness. God's silence is not indifference.

But His fatherhood means He governs people with patience that can feel unbearable to those who are hurting.

This is why human battles are rarely clean. There is no clear winner. There is no instant closure. There is often correction without restoration, truth without vindication, and healing that must occur without visible justice.

Understanding this does not remove the pain—but it prevents misalignment.

When you misinterpret God's posture, you may turn your frustration toward Him. Or you may take justice into your own hands. Or you may harden your heart against mercy altogether.

This is why strategy is essential.

Human warfare requires:

- Discernment to understand God's posture
- Restraint to avoid self-destruction
- Wisdom to know when to engage and when to release

Because when opposition has a human face, God is not absent—He is governing differently.

And until we accept that reality, every human conflict will feel confusing, unfair, and unresolved.

Privilege, Office, and Immunity in Human Conflict
Human warfare becomes most painful when ethics collide with responsibility.

There was an incident between two staff members under my leadership. The wrongdoing was clear. The team leader violated relational ethics. It was not a policy breach that could be documented or litigated, but it was a violation of human decency. The junior staff member was wronged.

That much was obvious.

What was not obvious to those outside leadership was everything else I had to weigh.

The team leader was an outcome driver. Her value to that shift and to the business was not easily replaceable. She functioned well with others. Her performance sustained operations. The junior staff member, though wronged, was not essential to the structural outcome of the business in the same way.

That is a bitter truth few understand unless they carry responsibility.

Leadership forces decisions that feel unjust on the human level but are constrained by function, sustainability, and consequence. I could not compromise the business outcome. There was no tangible policy violation that justified termination. What existed was relational misconduct, not procedural breach.

So correction took a different form.

I acknowledged the wrong. I apologized to the junior staff member. I provided training and corrective instruction to the team leader. I adjusted the schedule to preserve operational stability.

And yes—the junior staff member was the one moved.

Was she wrong? No. Was it fair? No. Was it necessary? Yes.

This is the kind of reality that overwhelms leaders—and wounds victims.

It reveals a hard truth about human warfare: outcomes are often protected over feelings. Systems prioritize function, not fairness. And those without the burden of responsibility rarely understand the cost of these decisions.

I have been on both sides of this equation. I have made these decisions—and I have been wounded by them. That is why this chapter is heavy.

Scripture does not shy away from this complexity.

Sarah and Hagar Sarah mistreated Hagar. Hagar was innocent in the conflict. Sarah held the position. And God did not remove Sarah.

Hagar fled because the relational environment became unbearable. God met her in her distress, affirmed her suffering, and promised her a future—but He did not dismantle Sarah's role in the covenant.

Why?

Because office carries consequence beyond conduct.

Sarah was the covenant carrier. Hagar was wronged, but she was not the one through whom the promise would flow. God addressed the injustice, but He did not redistribute the assignment.

This is one of the most uncomfortable truths in Scripture.

God sees wrongdoing. God hears the cry of the oppressed. But God also preserves structure, promise, and future outcomes.

That does not mean abuse is acceptable. It means correction is contextual.

In human warfare, office creates a kind of immunity—not moral immunity, but functional immunity. Some people are corrected quietly because public removal would damage more than it heals. Others are displaced because the system cannot absorb the loss of key contributors.

This is why human conflict is so dangerous.

You may be right and still be moved. You may be wrong and still be preserved. You may be wounded and still expected to heal without visible justice.

And this is where bitterness is born—if not handled carefully.

Understanding this does not make the pain disappear. But it prevents misdirected warfare. It explains why God sometimes meets victims in private while correcting offenders in ways we cannot see.

Human warfare requires more than righteousness. It requires wisdom under restraint.

And until this reality is acknowledged, people will continue to confuse God's governance with indifference, and leadership with cruelty.

Neither is true. But both are painful.

Moses, Aaron, and Miriam Scripture provides a striking example of how God handles wrongdoing differently based on office and consequence, not merely offense.

Aaron and Miriam spoke against Moses. Their sin was identical. Their words were equally slanderous.

Yet their outcomes were not the same.

“Then the anger of the Lord was aroused against them… and Miriam became leprous, as white as snow” (Numbers 12:9–10).

Miriam was struck with leprosy. Aaron was spared.

This difference raises an uncomfortable but critical question: Why?

The answer is not favoritism. It is office.

Aaron was the high priest. His public disgrace would not only have affected him personally; it would have destabilized the priesthood, disrupted national worship, and endangered Israel’s spiritual order. God could not expose Aaron publicly without far-reaching consequences.

Miriam, though a prophetess and leader, did not carry the same systemic responsibility.

Key Revelation Office carries immunity, not equality of consequence.

This does not mean officeholders are innocent. It means they are corrected differently.

Aaron was confronted. Aaron repented. Aaron pleaded for Miriam.

But his correction was restrained because his role could not be publicly dismantled without national cost.

Key Principle God corrects differently based on:

- Office
- Mandate
- Impact
- Consequence

—not merely based on offense.

This principle explains much of what feels unjust in human warfare.

Why some leaders are corrected privately. Why some offenders remain in place. Why some victims are comforted without public vindication.

It does not deny wrongdoing. It acknowledges governance.

This is why human warfare is dangerous. You may encounter injustice not because God approves it, but because removing a person would collapse something larger than the offense itself.

Understanding this does not excuse abuse. But it prevents misdirected warfare.

Because when you fight people without understanding office, mandate, and consequence, you risk fighting God's order, not just human wrongdoing.

When Mandate Shields the Guilty There are moments in Scripture that unsettle us because they expose a hard truth: mandate does not excuse sin, but it can delay, reshape, or relocate judgment.

This is one of the most dangerous realities in human warfare.

When people carry mandate, their failure does not unfold the same way as others'. God still judges, but He considers impact, timing, and consequence. And for those watching from the outside, this can feel unbearable.

Moses — When Calling Outlives the Crime Moses killed an Egyptian in anger. It was not accidental. It was not justified. It was murder.

Yet Moses was preserved.

Why?

Because God had already bound Israel's deliverance to Moses' life. Removing him would have delayed national redemption. Moses fled, was hidden, was processed in obscurity, and was later restored to assignment.

Moses was not excused. He was preserved for a future that outweighed the moment.

Judgment was deferred, not denied.

David and Uriah — When the Innocent Die and the Guilty Live This account should trouble us. If it does not, we have read it too lightly.

David abused power. He took another man's wife. He orchestrated that man's death.

Uriah was faithful. Uriah was loyal. Uriah died.

David lived. David's throne remained. David's lineage continued. David's mandate stood.

God judged David—but not in a way that restored Uriah.

The sword entered David's house. His family unraveled. His legacy was scarred.

But Uriah was still dead.

This reveals a painful truth: judgment does not always repair what sin destroys.

Mandate did not protect David from consequences, but it shielded him from removal.

And that reality should sober anyone who thinks human warfare is clean.

Ahab and Naboth — When the Righteous Are Crushed by Power Naboth did everything right. He honored inheritance law. He refused to compromise. He spoke truth respectfully.

He was falsely accused. He was executed. His land was taken.

Ahab repented—after Naboth was dead. God delayed judgment.

The dogs would later lick Ahab's blood, but Naboth was never restored.

This story forces us to confront a reality we avoid: sometimes righteousness does not protect you from loss.

God judged Ahab, but Naboth's life was not returned. Justice came—but not in time.

The Bitter Truth This Section Confronts You can be right and still lose. You can be innocent and still suffer. You can be wronged and still watch the guilty continue.

Mandate does not cancel judgment. But it can shield the guilty from immediate removal.

This is why fighting people is dangerous.

You may expect God to intervene swiftly. He may choose to preserve structure.

You may want vindication. He may choose long-term correction.

This does not make God unjust. It makes Him sovereign.

But it does mean this:

Human warfare cannot be approached with simplistic expectations of fairness.

If you do not understand this, bitterness will overtake you. You will mistake God's patience for indifference. You will internalize injustice as rejection. And you may turn your pain into rebellion.

This is why strategy matters more than reaction. This is why restraint matters more than outrage. This is why discernment matters more than emotion.

Because when mandate shields the guilty, the wounded must guard their soul carefully.

And this is where many lose the real war—not against people, but within themselves.

Human Conflict Inside Systems (Workplace, Ministry, Family) Human conflict rarely occurs in isolation. It unfolds inside systems—families, workplaces, ministries, and nations—each governed by structure, hierarchy, power, and consequence. Within systems, righteousness alone does not determine outcomes. Function, continuity, and survival often shape decisions more than fairness.

This is why human warfare inside systems is especially dangerous.

Systems do not respond primarily to morality. They respond to influence, alignment, and utility.

Cain and Abel: Conflict Inside the First Family System

The first recorded human conflict did not occur between strangers. It occurred within a family.

Cain and Abel brought offerings before God. Abel's was accepted; Cain's was not. Instead of addressing his internal posture, Cain turned his grievance outward and killed his brother.

God judged Cain, but Abel was still dead.

This account establishes a painful truth that repeats throughout Scripture: God's judgment does not always restore what human conflict destroys. Systems may correct the offender, but the damage done within the system often remains.

Jacob, Esau, and Rebekah: Dysfunction Within the Family Structure Favoritism distorted the family system long before deception entered it.

Isaac favored Esau. Rebekah favored Jacob.

Rather than confront the imbalance openly, Rebekah and Jacob resorted to strategy and deception. The blessing was secured, but the family system fractured. Esau's rage forced Jacob into exile. Jacob received the promise but lost proximity, safety, and peace.

This reveals another truth of system-based conflict: strategy may secure outcomes, but it often carries relational cost. Winning within a system does not mean escaping its consequences.

Laban and Jacob: Survival Through Strategy Jacob later entered another system—Laban's household—where exploitation was normalized.

Laban repeatedly deceived Jacob, changed his wages, and manipulated outcomes to his advantage. Jacob did not confront Laban directly. He adapted, observed patterns, and employed counter-strategy to protect his future.

Scripture does not condemn Jacob's response. It records it.

This account teaches that not all systems reward honesty with fairness. Some require discernment, restraint, and strategy for survival. Confrontation would have failed. Withdrawal would have forfeited destiny. Strategy preserved it.

Jonathan: Loyalty Conflicted by System Allegiance Jonathan lived within one of the most complex relational systems in Scripture. He was loyal to his father, King Saul, and covenantally bound to David.

Jonathan protected David, warned him, and advocated for him—but he never publicly broke allegiance with Saul. His loyalty was divided by system reality. He could not overthrow his father. He could not abandon David. He navigated ambiguity until his death.

This illustrates a painful reality in human systems: truth does not always grant freedom to act decisively. Sometimes integrity must operate quietly, within constraints.

Joab: Power Operating Beneath Authority Joab served under King David but consistently ran his own agenda. He killed Abner. He killed Absalom against David's instruction.

He maintained military strength while undermining moral authority.

David knew Joab was dangerous. Yet he tolerated him for years.

Why?

Because Joab held the army.

Removing him would have destabilized the kingdom. Justice was delayed for the sake of national survival. Joab's eventual judgment came later, under Solomon.

This account exposes a sobering truth: systems often tolerate dangerous individuals because their removal threatens structural collapse.

Prophets Against the One Who Speaks Truth Scripture records repeated moments when many voices aligned against one truthful voice.

Micaiah stood alone against hundreds of prophets who spoke what the king wanted to hear. The system rewarded consensus, not truth. Micaiah was imprisoned. The false prophets were honored—until reality caught up.

This pattern repeats in ministries and organizations. Systems often protect agreement over accuracy, peace over truth, and cohesion over correction.

Modern Systems: Workplace and Ministry Parallels In workplaces, employees may appear loyal while feeding information to competitors. In ministries, individuals may publicly submit while privately advancing personal agendas. Systems reward performance, results, and influence. Ethical violations that do not breach policy often go unpunished.

Victims may be acknowledged. Offenders may be retained. Adjustments may be made—not because injustice is approved, but because systems are designed to protect outcomes.

The Governing Reality of System-Based Conflict Human conflict inside systems follows a consistent pattern:

- Outcomes are prioritized over emotions
- Function is preserved over fairness
- Correction is contextual, not equal
- Victims are often required to heal without vindication

This does not make systems evil. It makes them limited.

Understanding this reality is essential for survival.

Those who expect systems to function like courts will be disillusioned. Those who expect righteousness alone to guarantee protection will be wounded. Those who refuse to discern structure, power, and timing will suffer unnecessary loss.

When conflict involves another human being inside a system, the fight is not only moral and emotional. It is structural, relational, and strategic.

Systems do not respond to righteousness alone. They respond to wisdom, restraint, influence, and discernment.

And if you do not learn how to navigate them with strategy, you will be wounded, weary, and eventually withdrawn.

Human warfare is dangerous not because people are evil, but because systems carry consequences far beyond individual behavior.

Understanding this does not remove the pain—but it prevents the greater casualty: the loss of your calling, clarity, and peace.

When God Shows Mercy to Those You Want Punished

Jonah and Nineveh To understand Jonah's resistance, Nineveh must be understood not as a generic sinful city, but as a symbol of terror, oppression, and historical trauma.

Nineveh was the capital of Assyria—the same empire known for brutality, humiliation of captives, mass violence, and psychological warfare. Assyria was not merely wicked; it was systematically cruel. For Israel, Nineveh represented the kind of power that erased families, displaced nations, and mocked covenant identity.

Nineveh was not an abstract enemy to Jonah. It was a historical threat.

Jonah likely grew up hearing stories of Assyrian violence. He would have known what Assyria had done to neighboring nations and what it intended to do to Israel. Nineveh embodied everything that endangered his people's future.

This is why Jonah's response cannot be reduced to prejudice or narrow-mindedness. His resistance was rooted in collective memory, national survival, and moral outrage.

Jonah did not fear Nineveh's sin. He feared Nineveh's escape from judgment.

"For I know that You are a gracious and merciful God, slow to anger and abundant in lovingkindness…" (Jonah 4:2).

Jonah ran because he understood God's character. He knew that repentance could neutralize judgment. And he could not reconcile that possibility with Nineveh's history.

In human warfare, this is a critical moment: when the offender is not just someone who did wrong, but someone whose wrongdoing has context, pattern, and scale. Mercy in such cases feels dangerous. It feels irresponsible. It feels like a betrayal of victims.

Jonah did not doubt Nineveh's guilt. He doubted whether mercy was safe.

God's mercy threatened Jonah's sense of justice, but more than that, it threatened his sense of security. A spared Nineveh meant a future Assyria. A future Assyria meant continued threat.

This reveals why human conflict becomes most volatile when mercy enters the equation. Mercy does not erase memory. It does not undo trauma. It does not guarantee safety. It only changes God's immediate response.

Jonah wanted finality. God chose repentance.

And this is where Jonah's warfare turned inward.

Jonah preached reluctantly. When Nineveh repented, he withdrew. He positioned himself outside the city, waiting—not for alignment, but for destruction. When judgment did not come, Jonah became angry—not at Nineveh, but at God.

This is one of the most sobering moments in Scripture.

The prophet who obeyed outwardly resisted inwardly.

Jonah's anger reveals a danger in human warfare: when God's mercy interrupts our demand for justice, unresolved pain can harden into resistance against God Himself.

God's response to Jonah was not punishment. It was exposure.

"Should I not pity Nineveh…?" (Jonah 4:11).

This question reframes the conflict. It does not deny Nineveh's guilt. It reveals God's sovereignty. It reminds

Jonah that judgment belongs to God, not to the wounded, not to the righteous, and not to the prophet.

Nineveh's repentance did not erase its future accountability. History would later show that Assyria's judgment did come. But it did not come on Jonah's timeline, nor in the way Jonah wanted.

This is the core lesson of this section:

You may be right about the offense. You may be justified in your fear. You may be accurate in your assessment.

And still be misaligned with what God chooses to do next.

Jonah teaches that human warfare becomes most dangerous not when evil prospers, but when mercy offends the wounded. At that point, the battle is no longer against the offender—it is against God's sovereignty.

Refusing to accept God's mercy does not protect justice. It risks forfeiting alignment.

Because when God shows mercy to those you want punished, the real question is not about them. It is whether you will trust God with outcomes you cannot control.

Discernment — Enemy or Misalignment? One of the most costly errors in human warfare is mislabeling misalignment as enmity.

Not every person who resists you is your enemy. Not every relationship that becomes difficult has turned hostile. Not every closed door is opposition.

Human conflict often arises not from malice, but from divergent assignments.

Misalignment occurs when two people are moving in different directions under different priorities, values, or seasons. Enmity, by contrast, is intentional harm—deliberate resistance aimed at sabotage, destruction, or displacement. Confusing the two escalates conflict unnecessarily and creates wars that never needed to be fought.

Scripture repeatedly shows that many conflicts were not born of hatred, but of purpose divergence.

Abraham and Lot did not part because they became enemies. They separated because the land could not sustain both of them. Moses faced resistance not only from Pharaoh, but from people who were simply not aligned with the demands of the wilderness. Paul experienced opposition not just from persecutors, but from co-laborers who were no longer assigned to the same path.

Misalignment requires discernment, not aggression.

When misalignment is treated as enmity, three dangerous things happen:

First, energy is wasted fighting people who are not attacking you. Time that should be invested in movement is spent in reaction. Momentum is replaced with defense.

Second, unnecessary damage is done to relationships that were meant to end quietly, not violently. Some connections are seasonal. When the season changes, forcing continuity creates strain and resentment.

Third, true enemies remain unidentified. When discernment is dull, real threats hide behind noise created by imagined ones.

Discernment asks different questions than emotion.

Emotion asks, Why are they against me? Discernment asks, Are they actually against me, or simply not aligned with where I am going?

Emotion seeks confrontation. Discernment seeks clarity.

This is why Scripture places such a high value on discernment. It protects against overreaction and prevents self-inflicted wounds. It helps identify whether a situation calls for confrontation, correction, distance, or release.

Some people must be confronted. Some must be corrected. Some must be limited. Some must be released.

Wisdom lies in knowing which response fits which situation.

Misalignment often reveals itself through friction, misunderstanding, or resistance to change. These signals do not always indicate hostility. They may indicate that the relationship has reached its limit. Forcing alignment beyond that point often produces conflict that feels personal but is actually structural.

Enmity, however, reveals itself through consistent patterns: deception, sabotage, manipulation, or intentional harm.

These require boundaries, strategy, and sometimes withdrawal.

Discernment protects from unnecessary warfare by helping distinguish pressure from persecution, difference from danger, and discomfort from threat.

Human warfare becomes destructive when people fight to preserve relationships that God is allowing to end, or when they pursue peace where boundaries are required. Both extremes lead to loss.

Discernment brings balance.

It allows peace without compromise. Distance without bitterness. Release without hostility.

This is why discernment is one of the most critical weapons in human conflict. Without it, people fight the wrong battles, exhaust themselves emotionally, and mistake transition for betrayal.

Not every opposition is an enemy. Not every ending is a loss. Not every resistance is warfare.

Sometimes, the most accurate reading of a conflict is not that someone is against you, but that the season of alignment has ended.

And recognizing that in time can save a life, a calling, and a future.

Deception Warfare — When People Manipulate Outcomes

Gibeonites Not all human opposition is open or confrontational. Some of the most dangerous conflicts arise through deception—when people manipulate perception to influence decisions, secure advantage, or alter outcomes without direct confrontation.

Deception warfare is subtle. It does not announce hostility. It presents itself as alignment.

The Gibeonites understood this well.

Faced with the advance of Israel, they did not fight with weapons. They fought with presentation. They wore worn-out clothes, carried moldy bread, and told a carefully constructed story designed to create urgency and sympathy.

Their goal was not debate or resistance. It was agreement without scrutiny.

Scripture records the critical failure:

"Then the men of Israel took some of their provisions; but they did not ask counsel of the Lord" (Joshua 9:14).

This single omission determined the outcome.

A covenant was made under false pretenses. Once sworn, it could not be revoked—even when the truth emerged. Israel was bound, not because the Gibeonites were righteous, but because leadership acted without discernment.

This account reveals a core principle of human warfare: deception succeeds when inquiry is bypassed.

Deception warfare does not rely on lies alone. It relies on:

- Timing that pressures quick decisions
- Emotional appeal that overrides caution
- Partial truths that sound reasonable
- Appearances that suggest harmlessness

The Gibeonites did not claim innocence. They claimed distance. They exploited Israel's assumptions and urgency.

And because leadership did not pause to seek divine counsel, manipulation succeeded.

This pattern repeats in human systems.

In workplaces, individuals may appear loyal while quietly advancing competing interests. Information is gathered under the guise of cooperation and later sold to competitors. Alliances are formed publicly while agendas are pursued privately.

In ministries, people may profess submission while subtly steering decisions, influencing narratives, or positioning themselves for advantage. Their resistance is not obvious. It is strategic.

Deception warfare thrives where discernment is relaxed.

Unlike open opposition, deception warfare often leaves the victim feeling complicit. Decisions were made willingly. Agreements were entered knowingly. Consequences feel self-inflicted.

This is what makes deception warfare particularly damaging. The injury is not only external; it is internal. Leaders replay decisions, question judgment, and carry the weight of responsibility for outcomes shaped by manipulation.

Scripture does not present the Gibeonite incident to shame Israel, but to warn future leaders: never allow appearance to replace inquiry.

Discernment is not suspicion. It is stewardship.

Human warfare requires pauses, questions, and verification. When decisions are rushed, flattered, or emotionally driven, deception finds access.

This is why revelation is a weapon. Not information—revelation. Revelation interrupts false narratives. It exposes motives beneath presentation. It reveals what is concealed behind politeness, urgency, or agreement.

Deception warfare cannot be defeated with confrontation alone. By the time deception is visible, agreements may already be binding. What is needed is preemptive discernment—the discipline of seeking counsel before commitment.

The Gibeonites were spared, but Israel paid a long-term price. The covenant reshaped labor, access, and obligation for generations.

This is the cost of deception warfare.

It teaches a final, sobering lesson: not every peaceful agreement is safe, and not every friendly approach is sincere.

When people manipulate outcomes, the greatest protection is not intelligence or experience. It is humility—the humility to pause, inquire, and seek divine counsel before acting.

Because in human warfare, deception rarely announces itself as opposition. It arrives disguised as agreement.

Special Weapons for Human Warfare The true victory in human conflict is not defeating another person. It is refusing to become a casualty of other people's internal disorders, unresolved wounds, ambition, envy, or of systems that reward function over fairness.

Human warfare is not won by spiritualizing people into demons. Nor can spiritual weapons be wielded carelessly against human beings without collateral damage.

Scripture consistently shows that when the conflict involves people, a different class of weapons is required—wisdom weapons. These weapons are developed earlier in this book and are echoed repeatedly in the Book of Proverbs, which serves as Scripture's primary manual for navigating human relationships, power, and conflict.

Several biblical tragedies make this painfully clear.

When Discernment and Revelation Are Absent Abel was righteous, but he lacked discernment about proximity. He did not perceive the danger in Cain's unresolved anger. There was no boundary, no distance, no restraint. Righteousness alone did not preserve his life.

Naboth was morally correct, but he lacked strategic protection within a corrupt system. He spoke truth, honored inheritance law, and still became a victim of power. Revelation might not have changed Ahab's heart, but discernment could have altered Naboth's exposure.

Uriah was loyal, honorable, and obedient. But loyalty without discernment placed him in proximity to a king who had already decided his fate. Uriah's tragedy was not a lack of integrity—it was the absence of strategic awareness in a compromised system.

These accounts are not indictments of the victims. They are warnings to the living.

Human warfare does not always punish evil immediately. But it does punish naivety.

This is why wisdom weapons are not optional. They are survival tools.

Discernment Over Reaction Reaction is instinctive. Discernment is intentional.

Reaction responds to what is visible. Discernment asks what is hidden—motives, patterns, history, and trajectory. Proverbs repeatedly warns that haste leads to error because speed in human conflict multiplies vulnerability.

Discernment creates pause. That pause is often the difference between survival and loss. It allows a person to recognize danger before it announces itself, and misalignment before it becomes betrayal.

Had discernment governed proximity, Abel might not have walked alone with Cain. Had discernment governed engagement, Naboth might not have stood exposed before a corrupt throne.

Silence as Strategy Silence is one of the most misunderstood weapons in Scripture. It is not weakness. It is containment.

Jesus demonstrated this when the woman caught in adultery was dragged before Him. Accusations were loud. Agendas were clear. The crowd wanted a verdict.

Jesus said nothing.

His silence dismantled the trap. It exposed motives without engaging them. When He finally spoke, His words carried authority because they were not reactive.

In human warfare, silence prevents escalation. It denies manipulators emotional fuel. It allows truth to surface without being forced. Proverbs teaches that restraint of speech preserves life because words, once released, cannot be retrieved.

Silence does not mean agreement. It means control.

Wisdom Over Confrontation Confrontation is often mistaken for courage. Scripture teaches otherwise.

Wisdom determines whether confrontation will heal or harden, correct or collapse a system. Many confrontations satisfy emotion but destroy influence. Proverbs consistently exalts patience, timing, and understanding over impulsive correction.

Not every wrong must be addressed publicly. Not every truth must be spoken immediately. Not every battle must be fought directly.

Wisdom preserves purpose when confrontation would destroy it.

Humility and Honor Humility is not passivity. It is strategic security.

People rarely target the humble because humility removes competition. It does not provoke insecurity. Proverbs links humility with favor, protection, and longevity—not because humble people are invisible, but because they are difficult to justify attacking.

Honor also restrains hostility. When a person refuses to posture, retaliate, or perform, they deny others the narrative needed to escalate conflict.

Humility is strength without exhibition. Honor is authority without aggression.

Boundaries Over Explanation Explanation invites argument. Boundaries establish clarity.

Human conflict intensifies when people feel entitled to reasons, access, and emotional availability. Proverbs teaches guarding the heart, not defending it endlessly.

Boundaries do not accuse. They do not debate. They do not justify.

They simply hold.

Boundaries could not undo what happened to Uriah or Naboth, but they remain essential for those who must survive flawed systems without absorbing their dysfunction.

Revelation Over Assumption Assumption fills gaps with fear and bias. Revelation fills them with truth.

The tragedy of the Gibeonites earlier in this chapter revealed what happens when decisions are made without inquiry. Assumption creates false peace; revelation exposes reality.

Proverbs elevates understanding above information and insight above knowledge. Revelation clarifies what appearance conceals. It reveals motives, timing, and risk.

Assumption reacts. Revelation governs.

The Nature of True Victory In human warfare, victory is not dominance. It is preservation.

Preservation of alignment. Preservation of integrity. Preservation of purpose. Preservation of peace.

These weapons do not guarantee fairness. They do not prevent all loss. But they prevent the greater tragedy: becoming hardened, reckless, or spiritually misaligned while responding to human conflict.

Human warfare requires restraint that feels counterintuitive and wisdom that feels costly. But Scripture is consistent: those who survive people do so not by overpowering them, but by governing themselves.

Because when conflict involves human beings, the greatest victory is not proving someone wrong. It is remaining whole while God governs what cannot be controlled.

Knowing When to Step Back and Let God Judge One of the highest expressions of wisdom in human warfare is knowing when not to fight.

Not every battle is yours to win. Not every conflict is yours to resolve. Not every injustice is yours to confront.

Scripture consistently teaches that some fights are not defeated by engagement, but by withdrawal, silence, and trust in divine judgment. This is not cowardice. It is discernment.

Human Beings You Must Never Fight Directly There are categories of people Scripture warns against engaging through confrontation, reasoning, or emotional reaction. Fighting them does not produce justice; it produces loss.

Never Fight People Who Carry Mandate or Authority Through Confrontation Authority introduces complexity into human conflict.

People who carry mandate—whether divinely assigned or structurally positioned—are not governed by the same rules of consequence as others. God corrects them differently, often privately, gradually, or later in time. Public confrontation of such individuals frequently backfires, not because they are right, but because their removal carries systemic consequences.

David understood this when he refused to lift his hand against Saul. Saul was wrong. Saul was dangerous. Saul was unjust. Yet David declared that judgment belonged to God, not to him.

This principle is not about endorsing abuse or injustice. It is about recognizing that confronting authority directly often destroys the one who confronts, not the one who is wrong.

When authority is involved, wisdom replaces confrontation.

Do Not Fight Envy Envy is irrational, obsessive, and relentless. It does not seek resolution; it seeks displacement.

Scripture never instructs believers to reason with envy. Envy cannot be corrected through explanation or appeasement. It feeds on comparison and thrives on proximity.

Those driven by envy will reinterpret facts, fabricate narratives, and persist even when proven wrong. The wise response is distance, not dialogue.

Envy is not defeated by winning arguments. It is defeated by removing access.

Do Not Answer a Fool According to His Folly Scripture gives direct instruction here:

“Answer not a fool according to his folly, lest you also be like him.”

A fool is not unintelligent. A fool is ungoverned—by emotion, impulse, pride, or rage. Engaging a fool pulls you into their operating system. Logic fails. Reason collapses. Outcomes become unpredictable.

Fools do not fight to understand. They fight to dominate, embarrass, or provoke.

Engagement legitimizes them. Silence exposes them.

Do Not Fight Angry People Anger escalates beyond logic. An angry person does not process proportionately. They act impulsively, then justify afterward.

Scripture warns that wrath leads to violence and destruction. An angry person can harm you and later explain it away. They may provoke conflict, trigger reaction, and then report selectively, framing themselves as victims.

Fighting anger head-on is dangerous.

The wise response is distance, delay, or withdrawal—not because anger is right, but because self-preservation matters.

Know When to Count Your Losses and Run Some battles are not meant to be won; they are meant to be escaped.

Scripture honors survival. David fled multiple times. Joseph ran from temptation. Jesus withdrew from hostile crowds. Paul escaped cities where staying would have cost his life.

There are moments when the most spiritual decision is retreat.

Running does not mean failure. It means discernment recognized danger early enough to preserve life and purpose.

Losses can be recovered. A destroyed life cannot.

Choosing Battles Is a Form of Wisdom Human warfare is not about bravery. It is about judgment.

Wisdom knows:

- When to speak
- When to be silent
- When to confront
- When to withdraw
- When to trust God with outcomes

God is not threatened by unresolved injustice. He is not pressured by your silence. Judgment belongs to Him, and timing belongs to Him.

Stepping back does not mean surrendering truth. It means surrendering control.

And that surrender is often the final weapon in human warfare.

Because some battles are not won by fighting. They are won by surviving, remaining aligned, and letting God judge what only He can judge.

Human conflict does not reward righteousness alone. It rewards wisdom.

Those who live long enough to fulfill their assignment learn this truth early:

the greatest strength is not knowing how to fight, but knowing when not to.

And sometimes, the highest victory is walking away whole while God handles what you were never meant to carry.

Chapter 12

When Satan Is the Opponent

This is both the easiest war to win and the easiest to lose.

It is the easiest to win because Satan does not possess independent power in the way many imagine. Scripture does not present him as omnipotent, sovereign, or equal with God. He creates nothing. He rules nothing by right. He governs nothing independently.

At the same time, it is the easiest war to lose because Satan is strategic, not powerful. He does not rely on strength. He relies on loopholes.

The Bible places far more emphasis on Satan's schemes than on his strength. He advances through deception, timing, and access, not domination.

He does not overpower. He maneuvers.

Most importantly, he rarely operates alone. His preferred battleground is not open confrontation, but human interaction. He capitalizes on human emotions, unresolved wounds, offense, envy, pride, fear, and conflict. He excels at turning people against people and then stepping back to accuse, distort, and amplify the damage.

Satan specializes in human-to-human warfare.

This is why spiritual warfare cannot be approached emotionally or impulsively. Discernment is essential. Misplaced engagement creates the very access Satan requires.

The Only Enemy Already Defeated—Yet Still Dangerous

When Satan is the opponent, the battle is not emotional, relational, or systemic. It is intentional, strategic, and spiritual.

This distinction is critical.

Many believers lose ground not because Satan is strong, but because the conflict is misidentified. People rebuke what requires repentance, confront what requires boundaries, and spiritualize what is human in origin. In doing so, they open doors that should have remained closed.

Satan is not God's equal. He is a defeated foe.

Scripture is consistent on this point. His defeat was secured through Christ. His authority was stripped. His end is already determined. What remains is not dominion, but limited operation within permission.

His danger does not lie in power, but in three areas:

- Ignorance — when people do not know who they are
- Access — when legal ground is given through sin, agreement, offense, or misalignment
- Timing — when fatigue, pressure, or transition creates vulnerability

Satan does not fight everyone. He targets those who threaten territory. Those whose alignment disrupts patterns. Those whose obedience closes doors he depends on.

This explains why spiritual resistance often intensifies at moments of clarity, obedience, transition, or advancement. The opposition is not random. It is calculated.

Satan cannot attack arbitrarily. He requires:

- Permission
- Agreement
- Legal ground
- Or proxy access through other people

This is why accusation is one of his primary weapons. When direct access is blocked, he accuses—before God and among people. When accusation fails, he provokes offense. When offense takes root, division follows. His strategies are consistent because they are effective.

This chapter clarifies four essential realities:

- Who Satan can oppose
- How he fights
- When he is permitted access
- What defeats him consistently

Spiritual warfare does not begin with studying Satan. It begins with understanding identity.

Those who do not know who they are fight defensively. Those who know who they are fight from position.

This is the governing truth of spiritual warfare: A defeated enemy is most dangerous to those who do not know he is defeated.

Ignorance gives him leverage. Fear gives him a voice. Misalignment gives him access.

But clarity shuts doors. Alignment revokes permission. Authority silences accusation.

This chapter is not written to magnify Satan. It is written to demystify him.

Because when Satan is the opponent, victory is not dramatic. It is precise. It is disciplined. And it is already within reach—for those who understand the rules of engagement.

Satan's Legal Framework — Access, Not Authority

One of the most dangerous misconceptions in spiritual warfare is the belief that Satan operates by power. He does not.

Scripture presents Satan as an accuser, a deceiver, and an adversary—not a ruler with autonomous authority. His activity is regulated. His movement is restricted. His reach is conditional.

Satan does not possess authority. He seeks access.

This distinction is foundational. Authority is granted by God and flows from position. Access is gained through permission, agreement, or legal ground. Satan cannot overrule God's authority, but he can exploit openings created by human behavior, misalignment, or ignorance.

Until this distinction is understood, spiritual warfare is approached incorrectly.

Authority Versus Access

Authority gives the right to command. Access gives the opportunity to operate.

Satan has no authority to command believers. He cannot force obedience. He cannot impose outcomes. He cannot override divine will.

What he can do is enter spaces where access has been granted.

Access is not power. It is permission—sometimes deliberate, often careless.

This is why Scripture does not command believers to overpower Satan, but to resist him, to stand, and to give no place to him. The danger is not Satan's strength; it is unguarded doors.

Biblical Pattern: Satan Must Request Access

Scripture consistently reveals that Satan cannot act independently. He must seek permission.

In the case of Job, Satan did not attack at will. He appeared before God and accused Job, questioning his integrity and motives. Access was discussed. Boundaries were set. Limits were enforced.

Satan could test. He could not destroy. He could afflict. He could not take Job's life.

The same pattern appears with Peter.

Jesus said, "Simon, Simon! Indeed, Satan has asked for you, that he may sift you as wheat" (Luke 22:31, NKJV). The request preceded the testing. The access was limited. And most importantly, Jesus declared that Peter's faith would not fail.

Even in opposition, authority remained with God.

Satan could shake. He could not own.

Jesus and the Limits of Satan's Power

When Satan confronted Jesus in the wilderness, he did not use force. He used temptation, distortion, and suggestion. Every offer was an attempt to gain agreement—an invitation to step outside alignment.

Satan offered kingdoms he did not own. He quoted Scripture he did not understand. He appealed to hunger, identity, and timing.

Jesus did not argue emotionally. He did not explain Himself. He did not negotiate.

He responded with truth and alignment.

Where alignment remained intact, access was denied.

How Access Is Granted

Scripture shows that Satan gains access through specific channels. None of these grant him authority, but all of them give him room.

- Sin — persistent disobedience that creates legal ground
- Unresolved offense — bitterness that sustains spiritual exposure
- Fear — prolonged anticipation of harm that weakens faith
- Deception — agreement with lies rather than truth
- Misalignment — operating outside God's order
- Ignorance — lack of knowledge that leaves doors unguarded

Ignorance is one of Satan's most effective entry points because it operates silently. A believer may be sincere, active, and devoted—and still exposed due to lack of understanding.

Scripture states this without ambiguity:

"My people are destroyed for lack of knowledge." — Hosea 4:6 (NKJV)

This verse does not blame Satan for the captivity. It identifies the cause: lack of knowledge.

Ignorance does not cancel salvation, but it compromises protection. It leaves believers vulnerable to accusation, deception, and unnecessary warfare. Satan exploits what is not understood—not because he is powerful, but because ignorance leaves doors open.

This is why Scripture places such emphasis on knowledge, understanding, and discernment. Not all captivity comes from rebellion. Some captivity comes from unawareness.

A believer who does not know:

- their identity
- their authority
- their boundaries
- their alignment

may unintentionally grant access where none was required.

This is why Scripture commands believers to *"give no place to the devil"* (Ephesians 4:27, NKJV). Place refers to access, not authority.

Accusation: Satan's Courtroom Strategy

When direct access is blocked, Satan accuses.

He accuses before God. He accuses through people. He accuses within the mind.

Accusation is designed to weaken confidence, distort identity, and provoke self-condemnation. Its goal is not truth, but disruption. A believer who doubts their standing becomes hesitant, defensive, and spiritually passive.

This is why Satan is called "the accuser of our brethren" (Revelation 12:10, NKJV). Accusation is his primary legal tactic.

Why This Framework Matters

Many believers attempt to fight Satan with intensity when what is required is alignment. They shout where repentance is needed. They rebuke where boundaries are required. They fast where understanding is missing.

Spiritual warfare becomes effective when access is closed. Closed access produces quiet victory.

When agreement is withdrawn, Satan loses leverage. When ignorance is addressed, exposure decreases. When alignment is restored, accusation collapses.

Satan does not retreat because of noise. He retreats because permission is revoked.

Until this framework is understood, believers will overestimate Satan's power and underestimate their position. Once it is understood, the war changes.

Because the battle is not about overpowering an enemy. It is about closing doors.

And Satan cannot operate where he has no access

The Primary Tactics of Satan — Scriptually Defined

Satan does not operate randomly. Scripture describes his methods as devices, wiles, and subtlety—not power.

The Bible repeatedly warns believers that ignorance of these tactics gives Satan advantage.

"Lest Satan should take advantage of us; for we are not ignorant of his devices." — 2 Corinthians 2:11 (NKJV)

His advantage is never strength. It is unrecognized strategy.

What follows are the primary tactics Scripture explicitly attributes to Satan.

1. Deception — Corruption of the Mind

Deception is Satan's foundational tactic.

Scripture establishes this from the beginning.

"But I fear, lest somehow, as the serpent deceived Eve by his craftiness, so your minds may be corrupted from the simplicity that is in Christ." — 2 Corinthians 11:3 (NKJV)

The serpent did not overpower Eve. He beguiled her.

Deception targeted perception before behavior. Scripture confirms this distinction:

"And Adam was not deceived, but the woman being deceived, fell into transgression." — 1 Timothy 2:14 (NKJV)

This establishes a governing principle: Disobedience is preceded by deception.

Satan does not begin with rebellion. He begins with mental distortion—corrupting clarity, reframing truth, and complicating obedience.

2. Subtlety — Gradual Misalignment

Scripture repeatedly emphasizes Satan's subtlety.

"Now the serpent was more cunning than any beast of the field which the LORD God had made." — Genesis 3:1 (NKJV)

Subtlety does not shock the conscience. It erodes alignment gradually. Satan rarely pushes believers into obvious error. He introduces small deviations—altered emphasis, delayed obedience, or misplaced confidence.

Subtlety reframes the question:

- From What did God say?
- To Did God really mean…?

This slow shift is what makes subtlety dangerous. By the time misalignment is visible, it has already taken root.

3. Accusation — Legal Warfare Before God and Man

Accusation is one of Satan's most explicit scriptural roles.

"For the accuser of our brethren is cast down, who accused them before our God day and night." — Revelation 12:10 (NKJV)

Accusation is legal, not emotional. It challenges legitimacy, standing, and worthiness.

This is illustrated vividly in Joshua the high priest:

"And he showed me Joshua the high priest standing before the Angel of the LORD, and Satan standing at his right hand to oppose him." — Zechariah 3:1 (NKJV)

Joshua was not being tempted. He was being resisted.

Satan positioned himself as an adversary in a judicial setting, accusing a representative of God's people. The resistance was not about Joshua's future; it was about his standing.

This reveals that accusation seeks to:

- Undermine authority
- Disqualify representation
- Interrupt assignment

4. Resistance — Strategic Obstruction of Assignment

Satan does not only deceive and accuse. He resists.

Resistance is not temptation. It is obstruction.

In Zechariah 3, Satan stood to resist Joshua's function as high priest. In another account, Satan directly influenced events surrounding David:

"Now Satan stood up against Israel, and moved David to number Israel." — 1 Chronicles 21:1 (NKJV)

This was not moral temptation alone. It was strategic provocation designed to produce national consequence. The act appeared administrative, even reasonable, but it violated divine order.

Demonic resistance often appears logical, defensible, and procedural, yet produces spiritual exposure.

5. Ignorance — Exploiting Lack of Knowledge

Ignorance is not neutral in Scripture. It is dangerous.

"My people are destroyed for lack of knowledge." — Hosea 4:6 (NKJV)

This destruction is not attributed to Satan's power, but to the people's lack of understanding.

Paul reinforces this principle:

"Lest Satan should take advantage of us; for we are not ignorant of his devices." — 2 Corinthians 2:11 (NKJV)

Ignorance creates access.

A believer may be sincere, active, and well-intentioned—and still exposed. Satan exploits what is not understood, not because he is powerful, but because ignorance leaves doors unguarded.

6. Fear — Undermining Confidence and Trust

Fear is a tactic Satan uses to destabilize faith and judgment.

Scripture is explicit:

"For God has not given us a spirit of fear, but of power and of love and of a sound mind." — 2 Timothy 1:7 (NKJV)

Fear pressures believers into premature action, unnecessary retreat, or compromise. It magnifies anticipated loss and minimizes divine faithfulness.

Fear does not require present danger. It thrives on projection.

The Scriptural Pattern Is Consistent

None of these tactics require Satan's authority. They require:

- Deception
- Subtle misalignment
- Accusation
- Resistance
- Ignorance
- Fear

Each tactic exploits permission, not power.

This is why Scripture does not command believers to overpower Satan, but to resist him.

"Submit yourselves therefore to God. Resist the devil, and he will flee from you." — James 4:7 (NKJV)

Resistance works because Satan's position is not dominance—it is conditional access.

Governing Truth

Satan's tactics lose effectiveness when believers:

- Understand truth
- Guard the mind
- Reject accusation
- Close access through knowledge
- Remain aligned

Scripture does not instruct believers to fear Satan. It instructs them not to be ignorant.

Because once his strategies are recognized, they lose their advantage.

Identity Warfare — Why He Attacks Who You Are

Satan's primary target is not behavior. It is identity.

Behavior can be corrected. Circumstances can change. But identity determines authority, posture, and endurance. This is why Scripture consistently reveals that Satan attacks who a person is before he attempts to influence what they do.

Identity warfare is strategic. When identity is unsettled, authority weakens. When identity is distorted, obedience becomes conditional. When identity is questioned, resistance collapses.

This is not a modern concept. It is a biblical pattern.

Identity Precedes Confrontation

Satan does not wait until a person sins to attack identity. He attacks identity at moments of clarity, calling, and confirmation.

This is evident in the temptation of Jesus.

Immediately after Jesus was publicly affirmed—"This is My beloved Son"—Satan confronted Him with a calculated challenge:

"If You are the Son of God..." — Matthew 4:3 (NKJV)

The temptation was not about bread. It was about sonship.

Satan did not question God's existence. He questioned Jesus' identity. He attempted to provoke Jesus into proving what had already been declared. Identity warfare always pressures proof instead of rest.

When identity is secure, no proof is required.

Why Identity Is the Battlefield

Identity determines:

- Authority
- Confidence
- Obedience
- Resistance

This is why Satan focuses on corrupting self-perception rather than forcing disobedience. If identity is confused, obedience becomes negotiable.

Scripture warns of this explicitly:

"For as he thinks in his heart, so is he." — Proverbs 23:7 (NKJV)

Identity warfare begins in thought and perception. When the mind is corrupted, behavior follows.

Accusation as Identity Erosion

Accusation is one of Satan's most effective tools in identity warfare.

He does not accuse primarily to expose sin, but to redefine the person by the sin. The goal is not repentance, but disqualification.

This is illustrated in the courtroom scene involving Joshua the high priest:

"And he showed me Joshua the high priest standing before the Angel of the LORD, and Satan standing at his right hand to oppose him." — Zechariah 3:1 (NKJV)

Joshua was standing in his office, not engaging in wrongdoing. Satan's resistance targeted Joshua's standing, not his behavior. The accusation sought to undermine his legitimacy as a representative.

God's response was not to debate the accusation, but to reaffirm Joshua's position and authority.

Identity warfare collapses when God speaks.

Provocation Through Identity Distortion

Satan also attacks identity by provoking actions that contradict calling.

This occurred with David:

"Now Satan stood up against Israel, and moved David to number Israel." — 1 Chronicles 21:1 (NKJV)

David was a shepherd-king, not a statistician. His strength had never been in numbers. The provocation tempted David to operate outside his identity—shifting trust from God to measurement.

Identity warfare often tempts leaders to abandon who they are in favor of what appears secure, logical, or impressive.

When identity shifts, exposure follows.

Identity Warfare and the Believer

Scripture teaches that believers are seated, called, chosen, and authorized. Identity is conferred, not achieved.

"But as many as received Him, to them He gave the right to become children of God, to those who believe in His name." — John 1:12 (NKJV)

This is why Satan's warfare intensifies when identity is clarified. He does not fight identity that is dormant. He fights identity that is active.

Those who do not know who they are may experience distraction or confusion. Those who know who they are experience opposition.

How Identity Warfare Is Won

Identity warfare is not won by assertion or argument. It is won by alignment.

Jesus did not respond to Satan with explanation. He responded with Scripture anchored in identity and obedience.

Joshua did not defend himself. God defended him.

David's failure did not redefine his identity because repentance restored alignment.

Scripture makes this principle clear:

"Therefore submit to God. Resist the devil and he will flee from you." — James 4:7 (NKJV)

Submission precedes resistance. Identity precedes authority.

Governing Truth

Satan attacks identity because identity governs authority.

When identity is clear:

- Accusation loses power
- Provocation fails
- Resistance collapses

When identity is confused:

- Fear increases
- Obedience weakens
- Access expands

This is why spiritual warfare does not begin with confrontation. It begins with knowing who you are.

Because when identity is settled, Satan has nothing left to negotiate.

The Battlefield of the Mind and the Word

Spiritual warfare does not begin in circumstances.

It begins in the mind.

Before Satan influences behavior, he targets perception. Before he pressures action, he seeks to corrupt understanding. Scripture consistently identifies the mind as the first arena of spiritual conflict.

This is why the Word of God occupies a central place in warfare—not as ritual, emotion, or repetition, but as governing truth.

The Mind as the Primary Battleground

The first recorded human fall did not begin with rebellion. It began with mental corruption.

Scripture states this clearly:

"But I fear, lest somehow, as the serpent deceived Eve by his craftiness, so your minds may be corrupted from the simplicity that is in Christ."

— 2 Corinthians 11:3 (NKJV)

The serpent did not overpower Eve.

He beguiled her.

The corruption occurred in the mind before it manifested in action. Perception shifted before obedience failed. Eve's understanding of God's word, God's intent, and God's boundaries was altered. Once the mind was compromised, the behavior followed naturally.

This establishes a foundational principle of spiritual warfare:

Satan does not need to control actions if he can distort understanding.

Scripture reinforces this principle:

"For as he thinks in his heart, so is he."

— Proverbs 23:7 (NKJV)

Whoever governs thought governs direction.

Strongholds Defined by Scripture

Scripture defines spiritual strongholds not as external demonic structures, but as fortified patterns of thinking.

"For the weapons of our warfare are not carnal but mighty in God for pulling down strongholds, casting down arguments and every high thing that exalts itself against the knowledge of God..."

— 2 Corinthians 10:4–5 (NKJV)

Strongholds are formed through:

- Imaginations
- Arguments
- Assumptions
- Narratives
- Repeated beliefs

They are sustained by agreement.

Satan does not require dramatic victories. He relies on repetition. When distorted thinking is rehearsed long enough, it becomes familiar. When it becomes familiar, it becomes accepted. When it is accepted, it governs decisions.

The Word of God as Governing Authority

The Word of God is introduced in warfare as truth authority, not emotional comfort.

This is demonstrated unmistakably in the wilderness encounter between Jesus and Satan. Every temptation was answered with Scripture. Jesus did not reason, explain, or defend Himself. He responded with alignment.

"It is written."

The Word was not quoted for reassurance. It was deployed to enforce truth.

Scripture declares:

"For the word of God is living and powerful, and sharper than any two-edged sword..." — Hebrews 4:12 (NKJV)

The Word discerns what emotion cannot. It exposes motives beneath appearances. It divides soul from spirit. It interrupts deception before it matures.

This is why Satan consistently attacks the Word—by questioning it, diluting it, reinterpreting it, or replacing it with experience. When the Word is destabilized, resistance weakens.

Knowledge as Protection

Scripture treats ignorance as a vulnerability, not a neutral condition.

"My people are destroyed for lack of knowledge." — Hosea 4:6 (NKJV)

This destruction is not attributed to Satan's power, but to lack of knowledge.

Paul reinforces this warning:

"Lest Satan should take advantage of us; for we are not ignorant of his devices." — 2 Corinthians 2:11 (NKJV)

Ignorance creates exposure.

A believer may be sincere, devoted, and active—and still vulnerable if understanding is absent. Knowledge in Scripture is not information alone; it is truth internalized and applied.

Where knowledge is absent:

- fear appears legitimate
- accusation feels justified
- deception sounds reasonable
- resistance weakens

Knowledge restores perspective and stability.

Renewal of the Mind as Warfare Preparation

Scripture emphasizes renewal of the mind as essential to spiritual victory:

"And do not be conformed to this world, but be transformed by the renewing of your mind..." — Romans 12:2 (NKJV)

Renewal is not passive. It is intentional.

A renewed mind resists deception naturally. An unrenewed mind requires constant correction. Transformation does not begin with behavior modification, but with mental realignment.

The Word accomplishes what discipline alone cannot. It restructures belief, clarifies identity, and anchors authority.

Governing Truth

The Word of God governs the battlefield because it governs the mind.

Where the mind is aligned, Satan's access collapses. Where truth is internalized, deception loses leverage. Where knowledge is present, ignorance cannot operate.

Spiritual warfare does not begin with confrontation. It begins with clarity.

And clarity is born of the Word.

Discernment — A Never-Ending Resource

Discernment has already been established earlier in this book as a core principle. It is revisited here not because it is new, but because its relevance never expires—especially when Satan is the opponent.

In warfare, repetition is not redundancy. It is reinforcement. Certain resources must be continually exercised because the cost of neglect is high. Discernment is one of them. When pressure increases, emotions rise, and stakes escalate, discernment is often the first discipline abandoned—and the consequences are immediate.

This section reinforces why discernment remains indispensable at this stage of engagement.

A Defining Example: Jesus and Peter

One of the clearest biblical illustrations of the necessity of discernment appears in Jesus' interaction with Peter. Peter made one of the most accurate declarations in Scripture: "You are the Christ, the Son of the living God" (Matthew 16:16, NKJV). Jesus affirmed that this revelation came from the Father. Yet moments later, the same Peter spoke words that directly opposed Christ's redemptive mission: *"Far be it from You, Lord; this shall not happen to You!"* (Matthew 16:22, NKJV).

Jesus' response was immediate and decisive: *"Get behind Me, Satan! You are an offense to Me, for you are not mindful of the things of God, but the things of men"* (Matthew 16:23, NKJV).

This exchange reveals a critical warfare principle: a person can be spiritually aligned in one moment and become a channel of opposition in the next—without becoming the enemy. Jesus did not label Peter as Satan. He addressed the source and intent of the statement. Discernment allowed Him to separate the person from the influence, revelation from resistance, loyalty from misalignment. Without discernment, this moment could have escalated into offense or relational rupture. Instead, clarity and alignment were preserved.

Discernment Applied: Correctly Identifying the Nature of the Battle

Every battle falls into one of four domains, and discernment is required to identify which one is in operation before any response is attempted.

Some conflicts are divine dealings rather than attacks. Jonah fled alignment, Saul resisted instruction, and Jacob wrestled with God—not Satan. These encounters required submission, not resistance. Scripture is explicit: *"It is hard for you to kick against the goads"* (Acts 9:5, NKJV). Fighting God only prolongs correction and deepens discipline.

Other battles originate within the self. Unresolved trauma, pride, fear, immaturity, and unhealed wounds often masquerade as external warfare. Scripture clarifies this plainly: *"But each one is tempted when he is drawn away by his own desires and enticed"* (James 1:14, NKJV). This domain does not require spiritual combat, but discipline, healing, renewal of the mind, and accountability. Rebuking the devil where self-governance is needed only delays growth.

Some conflicts are human—relational, systemic, or ethical. Personality clashes, workplace tensions, betrayal, injustice, and misalignment of purpose fall into this category. Scripture does not authorize believers to rebuke people as demons. Human conflict requires wisdom, boundaries, restraint, silence, and honor. Not every opponent is an enemy, and not every conflict is warfare.

Only when a battle is truly satanic does Scripture authorize spiritual resistance. *"Be sober, be vigilant; because your adversary the devil walks about like a roaring lion, seeking whom he may devour"* (1 Peter 5:8, NKJV). Satanic warfare is marked by intentional deception, sustained obstruction, accusation without evidence, fear disproportionate to reality, and erosion of identity and authority. This domain requires standing, resistance, and alignment.

The Cost of Mislabeling Warfare

Mislabeling warfare carries a high cost. It produces exhaustion when energy is spent fighting battles that were never satanic. It causes escalation when spiritual weapons are misused against human conflict. It creates exposure when unauthorized weapons open doors instead of closing them. Scripture warns against this error:

"The simple believes every word, but the prudent considers well his steps." — Proverbs 14:15 (NKJV)

Discernment protects energy, preserves authority, and prevents unnecessary wounds.

Discernment as a Tactical Discipline

Discernment is not suspicion. It is clarity under pressure. It involves slowing reactions, observing patterns, testing assumptions, distinguishing motive from method, and separating emotion from truth. Jesus demonstrated this consistently. He withdrew when confrontation would escalate, remained silent when speech would be weaponized, and engaged only when alignment demanded it. Discernment is the reason He was never manipulated into premature action.

Discernment is not a one-time insight; it is a never-ending resource. It must be continually exercised because pressure reveals what principles have truly been internalized. No battle can be won without discernment. It determines whether to fight, when to stand, when to withdraw, when to endure, and when to submit.

Without discernment, tactics fail—even when weapons are available. This is why Scripture places wisdom above strength and understanding above zeal. In warfare, accuracy precedes victory, and discernment is the weapon that ensures accuracy.

Authority and Posture — Standing, Not Striving

When Satan is the opponent, victory is determined less by activity and more by posture.

Scripture does not instruct believers to chase the devil, argue with him, or overpower him through effort. It consistently emphasizes a different stance—standing.

"Put on the whole armor of God, that you may be able to stand against the wiles of the devil." — Ephesians 6:11 (NKJV)

The emphasis is not movement. It is position.

Why Posture Matters More Than Motion

Striving creates exposure. Standing preserves authority.

Much spiritual defeat occurs not because believers lack power, but because they abandon position under pressure. When fear escalates, people rush to act. When accusation intensifies, they rush to explain. When resistance persists, they rush to confront.

Scripture calls this unnecessary striving.

"Be still, and know that I am God." — Psalm 46:10 (NKJV)

Stillness in Scripture is not passivity. It is confidence in position.

Authority Flows From Alignment, Not Effort

Authority is not self-generated. It flows from alignment with God.

"Submit yourselves therefore to God. Resist the devil, and he will flee from you." — James 4:7 (NKJV)

The order matters.

Submission precedes resistance. Alignment precedes authority.

Where submission is intact, resistance is effective. Where submission is compromised, effort replaces authority—and effort exhausts.

Standing Versus Arguing

Satan does not retreat from debate. He retreats from resistance rooted in truth.

Arguing engages his ground. Standing holds God's ground.

This is why Scripture never instructs believers to reason with Satan. It instructs them to resist. Resistance is not loud. It is firm. It does not explain. It does not defend. It does not negotiate.

"Resist him, steadfast in the faith..." — 1 Peter 5:9 (NKJV)

Steadfastness is posture.

Humility Strengthens Authority

Humility is not weakness in warfare. It is protection.

"God resists the proud, but gives grace to the humble." — James 4:6 (NKJV)

Pride creates exposure because it shifts dependence from God to self. When pride enters, striving follows. When striving follows, alignment weakens.

Humility keeps authority intact because it keeps submission intact.

Why Chasing Is Dangerous

Scripture never instructs believers to pursue the devil. Chasing suggests parity. Standing affirms superiority.

A defeated enemy gains advantage only when believers abandon their position and fight on his terms. Satan's goal is not to overpower believers, but to pull them out of alignment.

Standing denies him that access.

Victory in spiritual warfare is not achieved by intensity. It is maintained by posture.

Standing keeps authority intact. Submission sustains resistance. Humility preserves alignment.

When Satan is the opponent, the strongest position is not motion—it is steadfastness.

And when believers stand their ground, he has no choice but to flee.

Divine Silence — When God Withholds Speech to Secure Victory

Divine silence is not a vacuum. It is a strategy.

In spiritual warfare, silence is one of God's most effective instruments of victory. God does not always speak to accelerate movement; sometimes He withholds speech to exhaust opposition, protect purpose, and preserve the integrity of timing. Silence is not indecision. It is control.

Silence as Strategic Restraint

Scripture reveals that God often allows opposition to expend itself fully—running through every argument, accusation, and tactic—before He intervenes. This is not passivity. It is restraint designed to let the enemy overplay his hand.

The crucifixion stands as the clearest example. Scripture declares:

"None of the rulers of this age knew it; for had they known it, they would not have crucified the Lord of glory." — 1 Corinthians 2:8 (NKJV)

God did not clarify His plan. He did not correct the enemy's assumptions. He allowed silence to conceal purpose. The result was not defeat, but the greatest victory in redemptive history.

Silence prevented interference. Silence preserved destiny.

The Limits of the Enemy's Knowledge

Satan is not omniscient. He operates on inference, observation, and pattern—not full knowledge. This is why Scripture states:

"The secret things belong to the LORD our God..." — Deuteronomy 29:29 (NKJV)

Divine silence creates uncertainty in the enemy. When God does not speak, Satan is forced into guesswork. He moves without full information, miscalculates timing, and commits prematurely. Silence becomes a fog that disorients opposition.

What looks like delay to the believer is often confusion to the enemy.

Silence as Protection from Premature Revelation

God also withholds speech to protect people from revelation they are not yet mature enough to steward. Not all truth strengthens at every stage. Some revelation requires emotional stability, spiritual maturity, and disciplined obedience.

Jesus modeled this restraint:

"I still have many things to say to you, but you cannot bear them now." — John 16:12 (NKJV)

Silence, in this context, is mercy. It prevents misuse of insight, protects alignment, and guards against pride, fear, or misapplication.

God does not reveal everything immediately—not because He is distant, but because He is wise.

Why Silence Provokes Endurance

Silence exposes what governs the heart when reassurance is absent. It tests whether obedience is sustained by revelation or by faithfulness. This is why Scripture emphasizes endurance during delay:

"For the vision is yet for an appointed time; but at the end it will speak, and it will not lie. Though it tarries, wait for it; because it will surely come, it will not tarry." — Habakkuk 2:3 (NKJV)

Silence trains believers to stand without constant instruction. It strengthens internal alignment and deepens trust in God's sovereignty.

Divine silence is not a gap in strategy. It is the strategy.

It allows the enemy to exhaust his options. It conceals purpose until the appointed time. It protects revelation from immature handling. It strengthens endurance in the believer.

Silence does not mean God is inactive. It means He is controlling the field.

And when God finally speaks after silence, the outcome is already decided.

Victory Protocol — How Satan Is Ultimately Defeated

Victory in spiritual warfare is rarely dramatic. It is consistent.

Scripture does not present Satan's defeat as a moment of spectacle, but as the inevitable outcome of sustained alignment. He is not overthrown by emotional confrontation or occasional intensity. He is defeated when believers remain steady in truth, obedience, and faithfulness under pressure.

This is the protocol that governs lasting victory.

Victory Is Sustained, Not Sudden

Many expect victory to feel explosive. Scripture teaches otherwise. Satan loses ground gradually as access is denied and alignment is maintained.

"Resist him, steadfast in the faith..." — 1 Peter 5:9 (NKJV)

The word steadfast is decisive. Resistance that fluctuates invites re-entry. Resistance that endures closes doors permanently.

Satan does not retreat because he is confronted once. He retreats because resistance is maintained.

Truth Alignment as the First Line of Victory

Every satanic strategy depends on distortion. When truth is restored, deception collapses.

"And you shall know the truth, and the truth shall make you free." — John 8:32 (NKJV)

Truth alignment corrects perception, stabilizes identity, and removes internal contradiction. Where truth governs thought and action, Satan's leverage weakens.

Freedom is not produced by confrontation. It is produced by alignment.

Obedience over Explanation

Scripture repeatedly shows that obedience defeats the enemy more effectively than argument.

"To obey is better than sacrifice..." — 1 Samuel 15:22 (NKJV)

Satan thrives on delay, negotiation, and justification. Obedience short-circuits his strategy because it removes opportunity for interference.

Obedience does not require full explanation. It requires trust.

Endurance — The Weapon Satan Fears Most

Satan can endure rebuke. He struggles with endurance.

"For you have need of endurance, so that after you have done the will of God, you may receive the promise." — Hebrews 10:36 (NKJV)

Many attacks are designed not to overpower, but to outlast. When believers remain faithful under pressure, Satan's strategy collapses.

Consistency terrifies him because it denies him leverage through time.

Faithfulness under Pressure

Victory is secured when faithfulness is preserved, even when circumstances do not immediately change.

"Moreover it is required in stewards that one be found faithful." — 1 Corinthians 4:2 (NKJV)

Faithfulness keeps alignment intact during uncertainty. It ensures that when the season shifts, authority remains.

Satan exploits compromise. He is disarmed by faithfulness.

Governing Truth

Satan is ultimately defeated through:

- truth alignment
- obedience without negotiation
- endurance under pressure
- faithfulness in delay

Victory does not come because the enemy is dramatic. It comes because the believer is consistent.

When alignment is sustained, access is denied. When access is denied, resistance collapses.

Scripture does not command believers to overpower Satan. It commands them to remain steadfast.

And steadfastness always wins.

Knowing When the War Is Over

One of the most overlooked disciplines in warfare is knowing when a battle has ended. Many believers remain in combat long after victory has been secured—not because the enemy is still present, but because they have not recognized the signs of retreat.

Scripture teaches that Satan does not always exit noisily. Often, he withdraws quietly when resistance is sustained and access is denied.

"Submit yourselves therefore to God. Resist the devil, and he will flee from you." — James 4:7 (NKJV)

Fleeing does not always look dramatic. It looks like loss of influence.

Victory Is Discerned Before It Is Seen

Victory in spiritual warfare is often recognized internally before circumstances change externally. Peace returns before resolution. Stability precedes manifestation. Authority is restored before the environment shifts.

Scripture affirms this pattern:

"And the peace of God, which surpasses all understanding, will guard your hearts and minds through Christ Jesus." — Philippians 4:7 (NKJV)

Peace is not the absence of opposition. It is the presence of alignment.

When peace returns, the war is ending—even if circumstances lag behind.

Signs That Resistance Has Succeeded

There are clear indicators that the battle has turned:

Clarity replaces confusion. Fear loses its grip. Emotional volatility subsides. Decision-making becomes steady. Authority feels restored.

These are not psychological tricks. They are spiritual signals. Satan thrives on agitation and instability. When those collapse, his leverage collapses with them.

Why Continuing to Fight Becomes Dangerous

Continuing to fight after victory has been secured can reopen doors that were already closed. Over-engagement invites unnecessary focus on the enemy and distracts from forward movement.

Scripture warns against fixation:

"Forgetting those things which are behind and reaching forward to those things which are ahead." — Philippians 3:13 (NKJV)

Knowing when to stop resisting is as important as knowing when to resist.

Victory Is Confirmed by Stability, Not Noise

Satan's defeat is confirmed by the believer's stability. When reactions cease, clarity remains, and obedience continues without pressure, the enemy's work has ended.

This is why Scripture emphasizes vigilance, not obsession.

"Stand fast therefore in the liberty by which Christ has made us free..." — Galatians 5:1 (NKJV)

Standing fast preserves freedom. Chasing threatens it.

Weapons Authorized for Spiritual Warfare

When Satan is the opponent, God does not leave believers unarmed. Scripture authorizes specific weapons for spiritual engagement—but authorization is not the same as mastery. These weapons function effectively only within their proper jurisdiction and only when wielded in alignment.

The weapons authorized for spiritual warfare include the Word of God, the Name of Jesus, the Blood of Jesus, fasting, obedience, prayer (strategic, not repetitive), and the full armor of God. Each of these operates within God's order, not human impulse. They are not emotional tools. They are instruments of authority.

A critical distinction must be maintained: these weapons are effective against Satan, but ineffective—and often destructive—when misapplied to people. Scripture never instructs believers to rebuke humans, fast against relationships, or pray aggressively to resolve character issues. Misusing spiritual weapons against human conflict produces confusion, escalation, and exhaustion.

When rightly applied, however, these weapons do not amplify conflict—they deny access. They do not provoke engagement—they enforce alignment. They do not create spectacle—they sustain victory.

Understanding that these weapons are authorized is foundational. Understanding how they function, when they should be deployed, and why they work consistently is essential. That work requires depth, discipline, and training. That is the focus of the next chapter.

When Satan is the opponent: You do not negotiate. You do not reason. You do not retaliate emotionally.

You resist. You stand. You remain aligned.

Because the enemy is already defeated. The only question is whether you know it— and whether you will stand in it.

Victory is not achieved by shouting louder. It is secured by standing longer.

And when alignment is sustained, the battle ends— whether the enemy admits it or not.

PART IV

The Armor of God Reimagined

Chapter 13

The Armor of God — Identity, Position, and Authority

Understanding the Battlefield — Hierarchy Matters

Spiritual warfare is not chaotic. It is structured, ordered, and governed by rank.

Paul's language in Ephesians 6 is intentional. He does not describe a single, faceless enemy, but a layered system of opposition operating at different levels of authority:

"For we do not wrestle against flesh and blood, but against principalities, against powers, against the rulers of the darkness of this age, against spiritual hosts of wickedness in the heavenly places." — Ephesians 6:12 (NKJV)

This hierarchy explains why many believers experience unnecessary defeat. They engage conflict without discerning who is involved, what level of authority is required, or whether they are authorized to engage at all.

In warfare, intensity does not replace authorization. Courage does not override jurisdiction. Zeal does not compensate for rank.

Principalities function as chief rulers over territories, regions, nations, and systems. They do not operate primarily at the level of individuals, but over domains. Scripture offers a clear example in Daniel's encounter with the prince of Persia. The resistance Daniel faced was not personal opposition; it was territorial. Gabriel required reinforcement from Michael because the conflict exceeded his immediate assignment. Even angelic beings respect jurisdiction and rank.

This reveals a sobering truth: engaging territorial forces without divine authorization is not boldness. It is exposure.

Powers operate beneath principalities as enforcers. They implement and maintain agendas within systems such as economics, politics, religion, and culture. These forces do not need overt wickedness to succeed; they rely on structure, influence, and compliance. Jezebel's influence exemplifies this level of operation. Her strength was not physical dominance but manipulation, control, and access. Outcomes were shaped not by confrontation, but by influence over decision-making structures.

Rulers of the darkness of this world govern intellectual and moral climates. They thrive where truth is suppressed and confusion is normalized. These forces sustain deceptive philosophies, corrupt belief systems, and moral inversion. The Egyptian magicians illustrate this reality. Through occult power, they reinforced Pharaoh's resistance and sustained national deception. Darkness at this level is not emotional; it is systemic.

Spiritual wickedness in high places represents the most invasive form of opposition. These forces operate in the spiritual realm but manifest through oppression, torment, immorality, and affliction. Scripture records their activity through prolonged bondage and severe disruption—conditions that required direct authority from Jesus Himself. Not every believer is assigned to confront such forces without divine instruction.

Satan is not omnipresent. He works through hierarchy.

Each level of opposition demands discernment, timing, and proper authorization. Daniel's breakthrough did not come through impulsive confrontation, but through persistence, alignment, and reinforcement. This is why Scripture emphasizes prayer and corporate intercession. Some battles are not meant to be fought alone, because they exceed individual jurisdiction.

Many believers suffer not because the enemy is strong, but because they fight without clarity. Engaging forces beyond assignment produces exhaustion, frustration, fear, and unnecessary injury.

Wisdom in warfare begins with knowing what kind of battle you are in.

Before Paul introduces the armor, he clarifies the battlefield. A soldier who does not understand the structure of opposition will misuse his weapons, misjudge resistance, and misinterpret outcomes.

Standing effectively begins with discernment—not of strength, but of rank, authority, and alignment.

Why Armor Is Necessary Even From a Seated Position

Scripture declares that believers are seated with Christ in heavenly places. This position is settled, authoritative, and unquestionable. It is not aspirational language; it is a statement of present reality.

"And raised us up together, and made us sit together in the heavenly places in Christ Jesus." — Ephesians 2:6 (NKJV)

To be seated is to rule from a place of authority. In Scripture, those who are seated are not scrambling for access or negotiating power. They are positioned to govern. Yet the same passage of Scripture that affirms this exalted position also commands believers to put on armor. This raises a necessary question: if authority is already established, why is armor still required?

The answer lies in understanding the difference between position and posture.

Position speaks to where you are seated. Posture speaks to how you stand in that position.

Authority can be granted and still be poorly stewarded. Victory can be secured and yet be compromised through misalignment. The armor of God does not exist to elevate the believer; it exists to preserve alignment with a position already granted.

Satan cannot remove a believer from their seated position in Christ. That authority was secured through the cross and sealed by resurrection. However, what he can do is exploit access points created through deception, ignorance, fear, compromise, or neglect. He cannot dethrone, but he can distract. He cannot overpower, but he can destabilize. He cannot revoke authority, but he can erode posture.

This is why armor is necessary even from a place of victory.

Armor guards against erosion, not overthrow.

Scripture makes this distinction clear when it says believers overcome "by the blood of the Lamb and by the word of their testimony." The blood establishes legal victory. The testimony enforces lived alignment. Armor exists in the space between what has been legally secured and what must be practically maintained.

Many believers misunderstand spiritual warfare because they assume victory eliminates vigilance. In reality, victory increases responsibility. Those entrusted with authority must guard it carefully. A seated king still wears armor when entering contested territory—not because his throne is threatened, but because his authority must be enforced wisely.

The danger is not loss of position. The danger is loss of posture.

Posture is compromised when truth is loosened, when righteousness is neglected, when peace is replaced by anxiety, when faith is lowered, when identity is questioned, when prayer is neglected, or when watchfulness fades. None of these remove authority, but each one weakens its expression.

This is why Paul does not instruct believers to fight for victory, but to stand in it.

"Stand therefore…"

Standing is not passive. It is the disciplined maintenance of alignment under pressure. Armor makes standing possible without striving, reacting, or overcompensating.

The armor of God, then, is not evidence of insecurity. It is evidence of maturity. Only those who understand the value of their position will take the responsibility of guarding it seriously.

Authority is given. Posture is maintained.

And armor exists so that what was won through Christ is not diminished through neglect.

Armor Begins With Position, Not Combat

The Armor of God is not issued to people who are trying to win a war.

It is issued to people who are already positioned in victory.

Before Scripture ever speaks of armor, it establishes identity and placement. The believer is not fighting for access, striving for authority, or negotiating position. The believer's position is already settled.

"And raised us up together, and made us sit together in the heavenly places in Christ Jesus."

— Ephesians 2:6 (NKJV)

This is not symbolic language. It is positional truth.

To be seated is to operate from authority already conferred.

In Scripture, those who are seated are not retreating; they are ruling.

The Armor of God, therefore, is not defensive desperation.

It is positional enforcement.

Scripture does not begin with what you wear.

It begins with who you are.

You are seated in heavenly places.

You are positioned far above principalities and powers.

You are hidden with Christ in God.

You are authorized over all the power of the enemy.

"For you died, and your life is hidden with Christ in God."

— Colossians 3:3 (NKJV)

"Behold, I give you the authority to trample on serpents and scorpions, and over all the power of the enemy, and nothing shall by any means hurt you."

— Luke 10:19 (NKJV)

Authority is not something the armor produces.

Authority is what the armor preserves.

This is why believers who do not understand identity misuse the armor—reducing it to ritual instead of reinforcement, repetition instead of alignment.

The armor does not secure victory.

Victory has already been declared.

"And they overcame him by the blood of the Lamb and by the word of their testimony..."

— Revelation 12:11 (NKJV)

The blood establishes legal victory.

The testimony enforces lived alignment with that victory.

The armor exists to maintain what has already been won while operating in contested territory. It does not obtain authority; it safeguards posture.

If the enemy is defeated, why armor?

Because while Satan has lost authority, he still seeks access.

He cannot dethrone, but he can distract.

He cannot overpower, but he can deceive.

He cannot remove position, but he can erode posture.

The danger is not loss of victory.

The danger is loss of alignment.

The Armor of God is not a collection of spiritual metaphors.

It is a coordinated system, anchored in identity and executed from position.

Truth stabilizes identity.

Righteousness guards the heart and motives.

Peace preserves movement under pressure.

Faith neutralizes incoming attack.

Salvation protects the command center.

The Word enforces authority.

Prayer sustains alignment.

Watchfulness prevents ambush.

You do not put on the armor to become seated.

You put on the armor because you already are.

You do not wear it to gain authority.

You wear it to protect alignment with authority already given.

The Armor of God does not prepare you for victory.

It preserves you in victory.
That is the framework for everything that follows.

The Belt of Truth — The Structural Foundation

Paul begins the armor with truth because nothing else functions without it.

In Roman warfare, the belt was not ornamental. It was the structural anchor of the soldier's armor. Made of thick leather and reinforced with metal, it was worn at all times—even off duty. The belt secured the breastplate, held the sword in place, protected the lower abdomen, and signaled readiness for engagement. Without it, the soldier's armor shifted, weapons became inaccessible, and movement was restricted.

This physical reality is why Paul writes:

"Stand therefore, having girded your waist with truth." — Ephesians 6:14 (NKJV)

Truth is not one piece among many. It is the framework that holds everything together.

Spiritual warfare does not begin with confrontation. It begins with alignment. Truth aligns the believer with reality as God defines it. Where truth is compromised, the rest of the armor becomes unstable, symbolic, or ineffective.

Scripture defines truth in three inseparable ways. Truth is a person—Jesus Christ Himself. Truth is the Word of God. And truth is revealed and guided by the Spirit of God. These three never contradict one another. Together, they form the standard by which every battle must be interpreted.

This is why Satan's primary weapon is not force, but deception. Jesus called him "the father of lies" because every strategy he employs depends on distortion—of God's character, of God's Word, or of the believer's identity. If truth is loosened, resistance weakens without a fight.

Identity confusion always follows truth erosion. When the enemy questioned Jesus in the wilderness, the challenge was not about behavior, but identity: "If You are the Son of God…" Jesus did not debate identity. He enforced truth. Each response was precise, grounded, and aligned with what had already been spoken. Truth prevented identity from becoming negotiable.

The belt of truth serves the same function for the believer. It prevents circumstances, emotions, accusations, and pressure from redefining who you are. It holds righteousness in place, stabilizes faith, and makes the Word accessible. Without truth, righteousness becomes performative, faith becomes fragile, and Scripture becomes unusable.

Truth also brings stability. Scripture warns that a double-minded person is unstable in all their ways. Instability is not always emotional; it is often theological. When truth is mixed with assumption, compromise, or convenience, the inner life fractures. The belt of truth eliminates internal contradiction and restores coherence.

This is why Scripture exhorts believers to "buy the truth, and do not sell it." Truth must be possessed, not admired. It must be worn, not merely acknowledged. Like the Roman soldier's belt, truth wraps around the core of the believer's life and signals readiness.

Before the battle escalates, truth answers foundational questions: Who is God? Who am I in Christ? What has God said? What reality am I aligned with? When these are settled, the enemy's leverage diminishes immediately.

Truth is not optional. It is foundational.

Without the belt, the armor collapses. With it, everything else works.

The Breastplate of Righteousness — Guarding the Vital Centers

After truth establishes structure, righteousness provides protection.

Paul's sequence is intentional. The belt of truth secures the armor; the breastplate of righteousness guards what is most vulnerable. In Roman warfare, the breastplate was not decorative. It was forged to shield the soldier's vital organs—the heart, lungs, and major arteries. A strike to these areas meant rapid death, regardless of skill or experience.

This physical reality gives weight to Paul's words:

"and having put on the breastplate of righteousness." — Ephesians 6:14 (NKJV)

Righteousness, like the breastplate, exists to protect life at its core.

In Scripture, the heart is not merely emotional; it is the seat of will, desire, values, and decision-making. Solomon warned that everything that flows out of life originates there. If the heart is compromised, direction is compromised. If the heart is corrupted, destiny is exposed.

This is why righteousness is not presented as moral decoration but as protective alignment.

Righteousness, biblically defined, is not religious performance. It is right standing with God expressed through obedience. Long prayers, fasting, titles, and visibility do not constitute righteousness. Alignment does. Scripture makes this unmistakably clear when it says righteousness was credited to Abraham before the law existed—not because of ritual, but because he believed God and obeyed Him.

Righteousness guards the inner life because obedience keeps spiritual channels clear. Where obedience is present, accusation loses its power. Where compromise is hidden, accusation finds access.

The enemy rarely attacks openly at first. He probes for exposure. Hidden disobedience, unresolved bitterness, quiet pride, and tolerated sin become weak points in the armor. A soldier may appear fully armored, but an exposed chest is all the enemy needs.

This is why Scripture connects righteousness with boldness and stability. The righteous are described as bold not because they are fearless, but because their conscience is clear. Confidence flows naturally where alignment is intact.

Righteousness also preserves breath. In the physical body, damaged lungs result in suffocation. Spiritually, compromised righteousness restricts intimacy with God. Prayer becomes strained. Discernment dulls. Sensitivity to the Spirit weakens. The believer is not defeated, but slowly deprived of oxygen.

The breastplate is fastened to the belt for a reason. Righteousness cannot be sustained without truth. You cannot claim right standing while living in contradiction. Truth defines righteousness; righteousness expresses truth.

It is also important to understand that righteousness is custom-fitted. God's demands for consecration are not identical for every person. What preserves one destiny may not be required of another. Samson's consecration differed from Joseph's. Daniel's boundaries differed from David's. Righteousness is not imitation; it is obedience to God's specific instructions for your assignment.

When obedience is abandoned, the breastplate is removed. Scripture records this pattern repeatedly. Adam and Eve became exposed through disobedience. Saul lost divine protection when he partially obeyed. Samson's strength remained until he crossed the one line God gave him.

The cost of removing the breastplate is always higher than anticipated.

Yet where righteousness is restored, protection returns. Scripture records kings who appealed to obedience and received extended mercy. It declares that righteousness establishes a person far from oppression. It links alignment with favor, boldness, and longevity.

Righteousness does not make a believer perfect. It keeps a believer protected.

In warfare, survival is not determined by visibility or reputation, but by whether the vital centers are guarded. The breastplate of righteousness ensures that the heart remains aligned, the breath remains free, and the inner life remains fortified.

Without it, even truth cannot preserve you. With it, accusation loses access.

Righteousness is not optional armor. It is essential protection for anyone who intends to stand.

The Footwear of the Gospel of Peace — Stability, Readiness, and Movement

After righteousness guards the vital centers, Paul turns to the feet—not because they are less important, but because movement determines survival.

In Roman warfare, a soldier's effectiveness was often decided from the ground up. The footwear, known as caligae, was reinforced with thick soles and metal studs. These sandals provided traction, stability, and endurance over long marches and uneven terrain. A wounded foot could immobilize a soldier, leaving him exposed no matter how strong his armor or weapons were.

This physical reality gives clarity to Paul's words:

"and having shod your feet with the preparation of the gospel of peace." — Ephesians 6:15 (NKJV)

Peace, in this context, is not emotional calm or passive spirituality. It is readiness—the ability to stand firm, move deliberately, and advance without losing balance under pressure.

Peace stabilizes the believer in hostile terrain.

Scripture consistently presents peace as a guarding force. It keeps the inner life steady when circumstances are unstable. An anxious believer rushes, reacts, and misjudges. A peaceful believer discerns, waits, and moves with intention. Without peace, even truth and righteousness can be undermined by fear-driven decisions.

The gospel of peace also gives direction. It reminds the believer why they are standing at all. The good news of reconciliation through Christ is not only defensive; it is offensive. Wherever the gospel advances, darkness loses ground. This is why Jesus sent His disciples out with authority and why they returned astonished that demons were subject to them. Evangelism is not a side activity of warfare; it is territorial displacement.

Peace enables both resistance and advancement. It allows the believer to hold ground without panic and to move forward without compromise. Where peace is absent, progress stalls. Where peace is present, movement becomes sustainable.

The phrase "preparation of the gospel of peace" implies readiness. The soldier does not put on footwear in the middle of battle. He prepares beforehand. Likewise, peace must be cultivated before conflict arises. It is built through trust in God's sovereignty, confidence in identity, and assurance of purpose.

Peace is also protective. A believer who lacks peace is easily destabilized by offense, pressure, or uncertainty. Small conflicts feel overwhelming. Delays feel threatening. Opposition feels personal. Peace corrects perspective. It keeps the believer grounded when circumstances attempt to shift footing.

This is why Scripture repeatedly links peace with stability and endurance. Peace is not the absence of trouble; it is the presence of confidence in God's governance.

The footwear of peace ensures that the believer is not easily moved, easily tripped, or easily exhausted. It allows for long engagement without collapse. It protects against immobilization caused by fear, confusion, or discouragement.

In warfare, it is not enough to be protected from attack. You must also be able to stand and move.

Without peace, the believer stumbles. With peace, the believer advances.

The gospel of peace keeps the believer steady, ready, and mobile—able to stand firm when required and to move forward when commanded.

In contested territory, footing determines outcome.

The Shield of Faith — Mobile Defense Under Fire

After establishing stability and movement, Paul introduces the shield—not as a fixed piece of armor, but as a mobile instrument of defense. Unlike the belt, breastplate, or footwear, the shield is carried. It must be raised, positioned, and adjusted continually.

This distinction matters.

"Above all, taking the shield of faith with which you will be able to quench all the fiery darts of the wicked one." — Ephesians 6:16 (NKJV)

In Roman warfare, the shield was large, curved, and reinforced. It protected the soldier not only from direct blows, but from arrows, spears, and flaming projectiles designed to wound, distract, or disorient before close combat began. The shield was not optional. Without it, even a well-armored soldier was vulnerable at a distance.

Faith functions the same way.

Faith is not abstract belief or intellectual agreement. Scripture is clear that even demons believe. Faith, in warfare, is active trust—confidence in God's character, Word, and governance that is exercised in real time.

The shield of faith does not prevent attacks. It prevents damage.

Fiery darts come in many forms. Some are obvious—temptation, fear, intimidation. Others are subtle—accusation, delay, discouragement, unanswered questions, internal narratives that undermine confidence. These darts are designed to ignite anxiety, provoke reaction, or weaken resolve long before the believer ever faces overt confrontation.

Faith extinguishes these darts by refusing to internalize what contradicts God's Word. It does not deny reality; it denies distortion. It chooses trust over interpretation and confidence over speculation.

This is why Paul emphasizes the shield "above all." Without faith, every other piece of armor is exposed. Truth may be known, righteousness may be intact, peace may be cultivated—but without faith, the believer begins to absorb attacks that were meant to be deflected.

Faith is also directional. The shield must be positioned toward the point of attack. A lowered shield is as dangerous as no shield at all. This requires discernment—recognizing where pressure is coming from and responding intentionally rather than reactively.

Faith grows through use. Scripture records men and women who overcame impossible circumstances not because they understood outcomes, but because they trusted God in uncertainty. Faith is strengthened through engagement, not theory. Each victory prepares the believer for greater resistance.

Importantly, faith is personal but not isolated. Roman soldiers often locked shields together to form a protective wall. Scripture echoes this principle through corporate faith, agreement, and intercession. Some attacks are too intense to be absorbed alone. Community matters in warfare.

Without faith, the believer becomes vulnerable to fear and fatigue. With faith, endurance is sustained even when outcomes are delayed.

Faith does not demand immediate resolution. Faith sustains posture until resolution arrives.

The shield of faith allows the believer to remain standing under sustained pressure without being consumed by what was meant to destroy them.

In warfare, not every threat can be avoided. But with faith, no threat has to penetrate.

The shield does not eliminate battle. It ensures survival through it.

The Helmet of Salvation — Protecting the Command Center

Paul's reference to the helmet is deliberate and precise. In Roman warfare, a blow to the head ended the battle instantly. A soldier could survive injuries to limbs or torso, but a strike to the head was fatal. The helmet protected what governed everything else.

Spiritually, the same principle applies.

The helmet is not about appearance. It is about preserving the command center.

Scripture calls this piece the helmet of salvation, not because salvation sits on the head, but because salvation secures identity, authority, and orientation. When the mind is compromised, the entire life follows. No matter how intact the rest of the armor is, a corrupted command center neutralizes effectiveness.

Salvation is the foundation of spiritual consciousness. It answers the most important questions before warfare ever begins:

Who am I? Whose am I? Where do I belong? Under whose authority do I operate?

The enemy rarely attacks behavior first. He attacks identity. If identity collapses, obedience weakens. If assurance erodes, confidence disappears. If belonging is questioned, authority falters.

This is why salvation is constantly targeted—not the event of conversion, but the assurance and consciousness of it.

The helmet guards against internal erosion.

Accusation is one of the enemy's primary tactics. He reminds believers of past failures, unresolved mistakes, and former identities. These reminders are not meant to produce repentance; they are meant to produce paralysis. Condemnation does not correct—it immobilizes.

Salvation interrupts this cycle.

Scripture declares that there is no condemnation for those who are in Christ. This does not mean believers are sinless; it means they are no longer defined by sin. Salvation redefines the believer's standing even while growth and sanctification continue.

Another frequent assault is confusion. Confusion about calling. Confusion about worth. Confusion about purpose. Confusion weakens resolve and delays movement. A confused soldier hesitates. Hesitation in warfare is costly.

The helmet of salvation stabilizes identity by anchoring the mind in covenant truth rather than emotional fluctuation. It reminds the believer that salvation is not earned by performance nor revoked by pressure. It is a gift secured by Christ and sustained by alignment.

This does not produce complacency. It produces clarity.

Salvation also protects against deception. False doctrine, distorted truth, and subtle compromise often begin as ideas that sound reasonable but contradict Scripture. When salvation is not understood deeply, the mind becomes vulnerable to manipulation. The believer begins to negotiate absolutes, dilute convictions, or entertain narratives that erode spiritual authority.

The helmet preserves discernment by grounding thought life in truth already settled.

It is important to note that salvation is not merely an entry point into faith; it is an ongoing posture. Scripture exhorts believers to work out their salvation—not to earn it, but to live consciously within its reality. Neglect does not cancel salvation, but it weakens awareness of it. And weakened awareness produces vulnerability.

A soldier who removes his helmet in battle does not lose his rank—but he increases his risk.

Salvation protects identity. Identity preserves authority. Authority sustains victory.

When the command center is secure, decisions are clearer. Responses are measured. Fear loses leverage. The believer does not react to threats; they respond from truth.

This is why salvation must be worn daily, not remembered occasionally.

The helmet does not make the believer powerful. It keeps the believer sane, stable, and anchored in who they already are.

In warfare, clarity is survival.

And salvation protects the clarity that keeps the believer standing when pressure is relentless.

The Sword of the Spirit — Executing Authority, Not Just Defending Position

Every piece of armor discussed so far is protective. It stabilizes, guards, preserves, and shields. But Paul now introduces something fundamentally different.

The sword.

In Roman warfare, the sword was not symbolic. It was decisive. Battles were ultimately settled at close range, and without a sword, a soldier could not finish a fight. Armor could keep you alive, but only the sword could enforce victory.

Paul identifies this weapon clearly:

"and take the helmet of salvation, and the sword of the Spirit, which is the word of God."

— Ephesians 6:17 (NKJV)

This distinction matters. The sword is not merely Scripture known; it is Scripture wielded under the influence of the Spirit. The Word without the Spirit becomes information. The Spirit without the Word lacks legal grounding. Authority flows where both operate together.

The sword is not for display.

It is for execution.

Unlike other weapons, the sword requires skill, accuracy, and timing. An untrained soldier with a sword is as dangerous to himself as to the enemy. This is why casual familiarity with Scripture is insufficient for warfare. Reading the Word devotionally is vital, but wielding it strategically requires understanding, discernment, and alignment.

The enemy is not intimidated by verses quoted out of context. He is not threatened by volume or emotion. He responds only to rightly divided truth, spoken from position and obedience.

This is why Scripture records that Satan himself quoted Scripture. He did not invent lies wholesale; he distorted truth. His strategy is subtle—twisting what God has said just enough to produce misalignment. Jesus countered him not with new revelation, but with accurate application of what was already written.

The sword functions through precision.

The Word of God does several things simultaneously:

It exposes deception by dividing truth from distortion.

It penetrates internal confusion by discerning motives and intentions.

It enforces heaven's verdict in contested spaces.

But none of this happens automatically.

The sword must be trained into the hand.

Roman soldiers trained relentlessly with heavier practice swords so that real combat would feel familiar. In the same way, believers are called to study—not skim—the Word. Familiarity produces confidence. Confidence produces accuracy. Accuracy produces authority.

The Word is not activated by repetition.

It is activated by alignment.

This is why Scripture emphasizes obedience alongside revelation. The Word spoken without submission loses weight. Authority is not rooted in knowledge alone; it is rooted in agreement with what is spoken.

The sword is most effective when it is used sparingly and intentionally. Not every situation requires confrontation. Not every pressure requires declaration. Discernment determines when the sword is drawn and when it remains sheathed.

Jesus did not respond to every accusation with Scripture. Sometimes He spoke. Sometimes He remained silent. But when He spoke, it was precise, measured, and final.

The sword is not for argument.

It is for resolution.

The Word of God settles what emotions cannot. It clarifies what confusion obscures. It establishes boundaries where manipulation seeks entry.

In warfare, the goal is not to speak more.

It is to speak what heaven is already backing.

The sword of the Spirit does not create authority.

It enforces authority already granted.

When wielded rightly, the Word does not escalate conflict.

It ends it.

And when the battle is close, pressure is intense, and deception is subtle, the sword is not optional.

It is the difference between surviving the war and finishing it.

Prayer and Watchfulness — Sustaining Alignment and Preventing Ambush

Paul concludes his teaching on the armor of God in an unexpected way. After carefully outlining each piece of armor, he does not introduce another item of Roman equipment. Instead, he shifts the focus entirely:

"praying always with all prayer and supplication in the Spirit, being watchful to this end with all perseverance..."
— Ephesians 6:18 (NKJV)

This shift is deliberate.

Prayer is not another piece of armor. Prayer is the operational environment in which the armor functions.

A soldier can be fully armored and still be defeated if disconnected from command, unaware of movement, or inattentive to timing. Prayer sustains alignment. Watchfulness prevents surprise. Together, they ensure that the believer does not merely stand armored, but stands accurately.

Praying in the Spirit — Warfare Beyond Human Limitation

Paul does not simply say "pray." He specifies supplication in the Spirit.

This distinction matters.

Praying in the Spirit is not emotional prayer, eloquent speech, or extended repetition. It is prayer initiated, guided, and empowered by the Holy Spirit—beyond human intellect, emotion, or strategy.

Scripture explains this clearly:

"Likewise the Spirit also helps in our weaknesses. For we do not know what we should pray for as we ought, but the Spirit Himself makes intercession for us with groanings which cannot be uttered." — Romans 8:26 (NKJV)

Praying in the Spirit addresses a fundamental limitation in warfare: we do not always know what the battle truly is.

Human understanding is partial. Spiritual intelligence is complete.

When praying in the Spirit:

- Prayer bypasses ignorance
- Intercession aligns with God's will
- Strategy is downloaded, not guessed
- Resistance is met at its root, not its surface

This is why Paul emphasizes it. Warfare cannot be sustained by intellect alone.

Praying in the Spirit allows the believer to engage battles they cannot yet articulate, see traps before they manifest, and enforce victories that have already been decided in heaven.

Supplication — Precision, Not Generality

Paul pairs praying in the Spirit with supplication.

Supplication is focused, intentional prayer applied to specific resistance. It is not vague spirituality. It is targeted engagement.

Supplication acknowledges:

- There is real opposition
- There is a need for intervention
- There is dependence on divine timing and strategy

Jesus modeled this in Gethsemane. His prayer was not broad or ceremonial. It was precise, Spirit-governed, and aligned with the Father's will—even when that will involved silence, delay, and suffering.

Supplication in the Spirit produces endurance without collapse.

Watchfulness — The Discipline That Preserves Victory

Prayer alone is not sufficient. Jesus made this clear:

"Watch and pray, lest you enter into temptation." — Matthew 26:41 (NKJV)

Watchfulness is spiritual alertness. It is the discipline of observation under pressure—the ability to discern shifts, detect traps, and recognize timing before damage occurs.

Many defeats occur not because prayer was absent, but because awareness was lacking.

Watchfulness guards against:

- Premature confrontation
- Emotional reaction
- Misuse of authority

- Strategic exposure
- Delayed obedience

David survived Saul because he discerned danger early and withdrew wisely. Jesus avoided countless traps because He perceived intent before responding. Paul escaped assassination plots because intelligence preceded movement.

Watchfulness keeps the believer one step ahead.

Why Prayer in the Spirit Must Be Continuous

Warfare is not seasonal. Neither is opposition.

Paul writes, “Praying always.”

The enemy consults continuously. Strategies are sustained, not improvised. This is why praying in the Spirit cannot be occasional or reactionary. It must be continual.

Praying in the Spirit:

- Maintains alignment
- Preserves sensitivity
- Prevents spiritual fatigue
- Keeps posture accurate

When prayer weakens, the armor loses coordination. When watchfulness fades, even the armored become vulnerable.

The Final Function of Prayer in Warfare

Prayer does not inform God of battle. It positions the believer within divine strategy.

Praying in the Spirit does not convince God to act. It aligns the believer with what God has already authorized.

Watchfulness ensures that response, timing, and restraint remain accurate.

This is why Paul ends the armor discussion here—not with another weapon, but with a posture.

Because in warfare:

- Armor protects
- The Word enforces
- Prayer sustains
- Watchfulness preserves

And praying in the Spirit is what keeps all of them functioning together.

When prayer in the Spirit and watchfulness operate together, the believer does not strive, panic, or overreact.

They remain standing— until the enemy withdraws.

Chapter 14

Sharpening Your Weapons — Tactical Readiness

Victory is not seasonal. Readiness must be continuous.

Wars are not lost in combat. They are lost in neglect before engagement.

This chapter serves as the commissioning moment of this book. Everything discussed so far—discernment, alignment, silence, wisdom, authority, posture, and the armor of God—finds its practical convergence here. The aim is not to teach new tactics, but to establish a sustaining posture: a life that remains prepared before pressure arrives.

Readiness is not an emotional state. It is not intensity, urgency, or reaction. Readiness is a discipline—quiet, deliberate, and maintained over time. It is the condition of a person who understands that warfare is not episodic but continual, and that consistency, not drama, determines longevity.

Weapons dull when they are admired but not used. Discernment weakens when it is assumed rather than exercised. Alignment erodes when familiarity replaces vigilance. Many defeats attributed to opposition are, in reality, the result of neglect—small compromises in preparation that accumulate long before engagement begins.

Tactical readiness means living in such a way that when conflict arises, nothing needs to be assembled. There is no scrambling for clarity, no searching for posture, no confusion about authority. The response is steady because preparation has already been done.

The central truth of warfare remains unchanged: war is won before the first shot is fired. Outcomes are decided in advance—by habits, by priorities, by discipline, and by the choices made when no one is watching and no battle is visible.

This chapter does not call for more effort. It calls for sustained alignment. It does not urge reaction. It commissions responsibility. The goal is not survival, but dominion through consistency.

From here, the focus narrows to what keeps a believer ready—how weapons are sharpened, how discernment is trained, and how posture is preserved so that victory remains uninterrupted.

Readiness Is a Discipline, Not a Moment

Readiness is not an event that occurs when pressure arrives. It is a condition cultivated long before opposition becomes visible. In warfare, those who wait to prepare until conflict begins are already behind. Readiness is established through habits, reinforced through consistency, and preserved through vigilance.

Spiritual fitness does not maintain itself. It requires intentional upkeep.

Many losses in warfare are not caused by the strength of the enemy but by the assumption of readiness. Familiarity breeds carelessness. Confidence without maintenance leads to exposure. What once required discipline is taken for granted, and what is taken for granted is rarely protected.

Readiness is demonstrated in the unseen decisions of daily life. It is reflected in how consistently truth is reinforced, how obedience is sustained without supervision, how emotional responses are regulated, and how attentiveness is preserved even when nothing appears urgent. These quiet disciplines determine whether a person remains steady when pressure arrives.

War is not won in the moment of engagement. It is won in the long, uneventful seasons where preparation either continues or quietly stops. Those who endure are not those who react the fastest, but those who remain the most prepared.

Keeping Your Weapons Sharp

Weapons do not remain effective by default. Sharpness is the result of deliberate and repeated maintenance. Even the most advanced weapon fails if it is neglected, and even the most skilled soldier is vulnerable when their tools are dull. In warfare, effectiveness is not measured by possession, but by condition.

Spiritual weapons are sharpened through consistency, not intensity. Truth must be reinforced regularly or it becomes abstract. Obedience must be practiced continually or it weakens into selective compliance. Spiritual disciplines must be sustained over time or they deteriorate into occasional performance. Emotional regulation must be exercised intentionally or reactions begin to govern decisions. Discernment must be trained deliberately or perception becomes clouded.

Sharpness is preserved through repetition. What is revisited remains accessible. What is neglected becomes unreliable under pressure. Many failures attributed to external opposition are, in reality, the result of internal dullness—truth once known but no longer reinforced, convictions once held but no longer practiced, disciplines once valued but now inconsistently applied.

A dull weapon does not fail loudly. It fails gradually. Precision is lost first, then confidence, and finally effectiveness. When pressure arrives, the deficiency becomes visible, not because the battle is unusual, but because preparation has quietly declined.

Keeping weapons sharp requires routine attention, not crisis-driven urgency. It is the discipline of returning to foundational practices even when progress feels slow and opposition is absent. Those who remain effective in warfare are not those who discover new weapons in moments of crisis, but those who faithfully maintain what they already have.

Sharpness is not about readiness for spectacle. It is about reliability under pressure.

Training Discernment Daily

Discernment is not instinct, intuition, or personality. It is trained perception. It develops through deliberate attention, repeated practice, and disciplined restraint. Those who endure in warfare are not distinguished by faster reactions, louder responses, or stronger emotions. They are distinguished by clarity.

Discernment sharpens the ability to distinguish between what is urgent and what is important, what is threatening and what is distracting, what requires engagement and what requires restraint. Without trained discernment, strength is misapplied, energy is wasted, and authority is diluted through unnecessary conflict.

Daily training in discernment involves slowing responses rather than accelerating them. It requires observing patterns instead of reacting to incidents, testing assumptions instead of defending impressions, and separating emotional stimulation from strategic relevance. Clarity is rarely produced by speed. It is produced by attentiveness.

Untrained discernment defaults to reaction. Trained discernment chooses response. Reaction is driven by emotion and immediacy. Response is governed by purpose and timing. The difference determines whether a situation escalates or resolves, whether authority is preserved or compromised.

Discernment must be exercised in ordinary moments, not reserved for visible conflict. Small decisions, minor provocations, and routine interactions are the training ground. What is practiced there determines performance when pressure increases.

Those who survive warfare do not see more information than others. They see meaning more accurately. Clear perception prevents unnecessary battles, preserves focus, and protects alignment. In warfare, clarity is not optional. It is decisive.

Choosing Your Battles Wisely

Not every opponent is your assignment. Not every provocation warrants engagement.

Wisdom in warfare is not only knowing how to fight; it is knowing what deserves your strength.

Strategic readiness requires selectivity. Energy is finite, focus is fragile, and authority is compromised when attention is scattered. Those who carry responsibility must learn restraint—not as avoidance, but as prioritization. The discipline to disengage from distractions is as critical as the courage to confront genuine threats.

Battle selection is governed by three essential questions:

Who to fight. Discern the difference between true opposition and temporary instruments. Not every resistance is hostile, and not every challenge is adversarial. Engaging the wrong target expends strength without advancing purpose.

When to fight. Timing determines legitimacy. Even a justified engagement can fail if entered prematurely or pursued too late. Strategic patience preserves authority; impulsive action weakens it.

What to fight for—and what to let go. Not every issue deserves escalation. Some confrontations drain focus without yielding progress. Strength must be reserved for matters that affect assignment, alignment, and future impact.

There are conflicts that are not worth engaging because they offer no meaningful gain. Those with nothing to lose can afford chaos; those with purpose cannot. Strategic wisdom refuses to be drawn into exchanges that diminish focus or compromise trajectory.

Choosing battles wisely is not disengagement from responsibility. It is stewardship of strength. The disciplined refusal to respond to every stimulus preserves clarity, protects momentum, and sustains readiness for the engagements that truly matter.

Timing as a Weapon

Timing is not a secondary consideration in warfare. It is a weapon in itself. A correct action taken at the wrong time can be as damaging as a wrong action taken deliberately. Strategic readiness requires sensitivity not only to what must be done, but when it must be done.

There are seasons for engagement and seasons for restraint. Movement outside of timing weakens authority and exposes position. Action taken without timing forfeits legitimacy, even when the cause appears justified. In warfare, haste often masquerades as courage, while patience is misread as fear. In reality, timing distinguishes wisdom from impulse.

Poor timing exhausts resources prematurely. It provokes resistance before alignment is secured and invites consequences before capacity is built. Strategic timing, on the other hand, consolidates strength, preserves credibility, and ensures that effort produces outcome rather than regret.

Readiness does not mean constant engagement. It means constant discernment. The disciplined ability to wait, to hold position, and to advance only when alignment and timing converge is a mark of maturity in warfare. Those who endure are not those who act at every opportunity, but those who act at the right moment.

Timing protects future gains. It prevents unnecessary loss, preserves momentum, and allows engagement to occur with clarity rather than compulsion. In warfare, knowing when not to fight is as powerful as knowing how to fight.

Timing is not delay for its own sake. It is strategic restraint that preserves victory.

Warfare Requires Support, Not Isolation

No sustained warfare is fought alone. Isolation weakens judgment, narrows perspective, and accelerates fatigue. Readiness is preserved through structure, covering, and shared responsibility. Strength multiplies when support systems are intentional rather than incidental.

Scripture consistently affirms this principle. Strength increases through alignment, not separation. One may pursue limited ground alone, but joined strength expands reach exponentially. Two aligned individuals carry far more impact than isolated effort, and unity creates durability that isolation cannot sustain. What stands alone is easily strained; what is joined is reinforced.

Support is not weakness. It is strategy. Warfare demands capacity, and capacity is preserved through shared strength.

Alignment with others stabilizes focus, protects rhythm, and reinforces clarity. Isolation may feel efficient in the short term, but over time it erodes endurance and increases vulnerability.

Support takes different forms depending on season and assignment. Sometimes it is intercession—others standing watch while focus is directed elsewhere. Sometimes it is counsel—trusted voices that expose blind spots and prevent drift. Sometimes it is practical reinforcement—delegation, rest, or logistical help that preserves energy for essential engagements. Each form serves the same purpose: sustaining readiness without exhaustion.

Effective support is not about dependency. It is about distribution. Responsibility shared appropriately prevents overload and preserves precision. When every task, decision, and burden is carried alone, clarity diminishes and reaction replaces strategy.

Readiness is not proven by how much one can carry alone. It is proven by how wisely strength is multiplied. Warfare favors alignment. Stability increases where connection is intentional. Endurance is strongest where support is present.

Isolation drains. Alignment fortifies. And sustained victory belongs to those who understand the power of standing together.

Framework One — Urgent vs. Important

Not every battle carries the same weight. Some demand immediate action; others only demand attention because they are loud. Without a framework for prioritization, warfare becomes reactive, exhausting, and inefficient. Strategic readiness requires the ability to distinguish urgency from importance.

Urgent battles create pressure. They demand attention, provoke emotion, and often feel unavoidable. Important battles, however, shape outcomes. They determine direction, longevity, and future stability. When urgency is allowed to override importance, energy is spent managing noise while core issues remain unresolved.

There are battles that are both important and urgent. These threaten trajectory and require immediate engagement. Delay in these moments produces loss that cannot be easily recovered. There are also battles that are important but not urgent. These require planning, patience, and deliberate strategy rather than emotional response. Mishandling these through haste often creates complications that could have been avoided.

Some battles are urgent but not important. They appear pressing, demand reaction, and generate distraction, yet contribute nothing to long-term purpose. These are among the most dangerous because they consume attention while offering no return. Engaging them drains strength without advancing position.

Finally, there are battles that are neither urgent nor important. These add no value, produce no growth, and do not affect outcome. Engaging them is pure loss—of time, focus, and emotional capacity.

Wisdom in warfare is the discipline of categorization. Emotion reacts to urgency; discernment prioritizes importance. Strategic readiness depends on the ability to pause, assess, and choose engagement based on consequence rather than pressure.

When priorities are clear, strength is preserved. When priorities are confused, even legitimate battles become costly. Victory is sustained not by fighting more, but by fighting what matters.

Framework Two — Temporal vs. Destiny / Eternity

Not all battles are equal because not all outcomes carry the same weight. Strategic readiness requires a second filter—one that distinguishes between what is temporary and what is eternal. Without this framework, energy is easily spent protecting what will not last while neglecting what truly matters.

Temporal battles are tied to immediate comfort, recognition, emotion, or convenience. They often feel pressing, personal, and justified, yet their impact fades quickly. Destiny and eternity, however, are non-negotiable. What affects purpose, alignment, legacy, and eternal standing must always take precedence over what merely satisfies the moment.

When temporal concerns compete with destiny, one must yield. Desire cannot outrank assignment. Preference cannot override purpose. Readiness is compromised whenever short-term gain is allowed to jeopardize long-term calling. Strategic warfare demands the discipline to release what feels urgent if it threatens what is essential.

This framework simplifies decision-making. If a battle threatens destiny or eternal alignment, it must be engaged with seriousness and resolve. If it only feeds appetite, ego, fear, or insecurity, it must be released—regardless of how justified it appears. Strength preserved through restraint is often more powerful than strength expended in reaction.

Destiny and desire cannot coexist as equals. One will always dominate the other. Tactical readiness is demonstrated by the ability to choose alignment over impulse and eternity over immediacy. When decisions are filtered through this lens, warfare becomes clearer, focus is preserved, and victory remains intact.

The battles that matter most are not always the loudest. They are the ones whose outcomes extend beyond the present moment.

Final Governing Truth of the Book

You do not fight to win. You fight from victory.

Warfare is not the pursuit of authority; it is the preservation of alignment with authority already given. The posture of victory precedes every legitimate engagement. Striving weakens position. Standing preserves it.

You do not prepare when war arrives. You prepare so that when it does, nothing shifts.

Readiness is not reactive. It is sustained. It is the result of discipline maintained in quiet seasons, alignment guarded in ordinary moments, and discernment trained long before pressure appears. What holds under fire is what has been reinforced consistently.

Authority does not increase in conflict. It is revealed there.

Those who endure are not those who fight the hardest, but those who remain unmoved—clear in purpose, steady in posture, and disciplined in engagement. Victory is sustained through consistency, not intensity.

This book has not been about confrontation for its own sake. It has been about clarity. Not about aggression, but about alignment. Not about winning every battle, but about preserving destiny.

When warfare is approached this way, conflict no longer destabilizes. Pressure no longer dictates response. And opposition no longer determines direction.

You remain positioned. You remain aligned. You remain ready.

That is tactical readiness. That is dominion sustained.

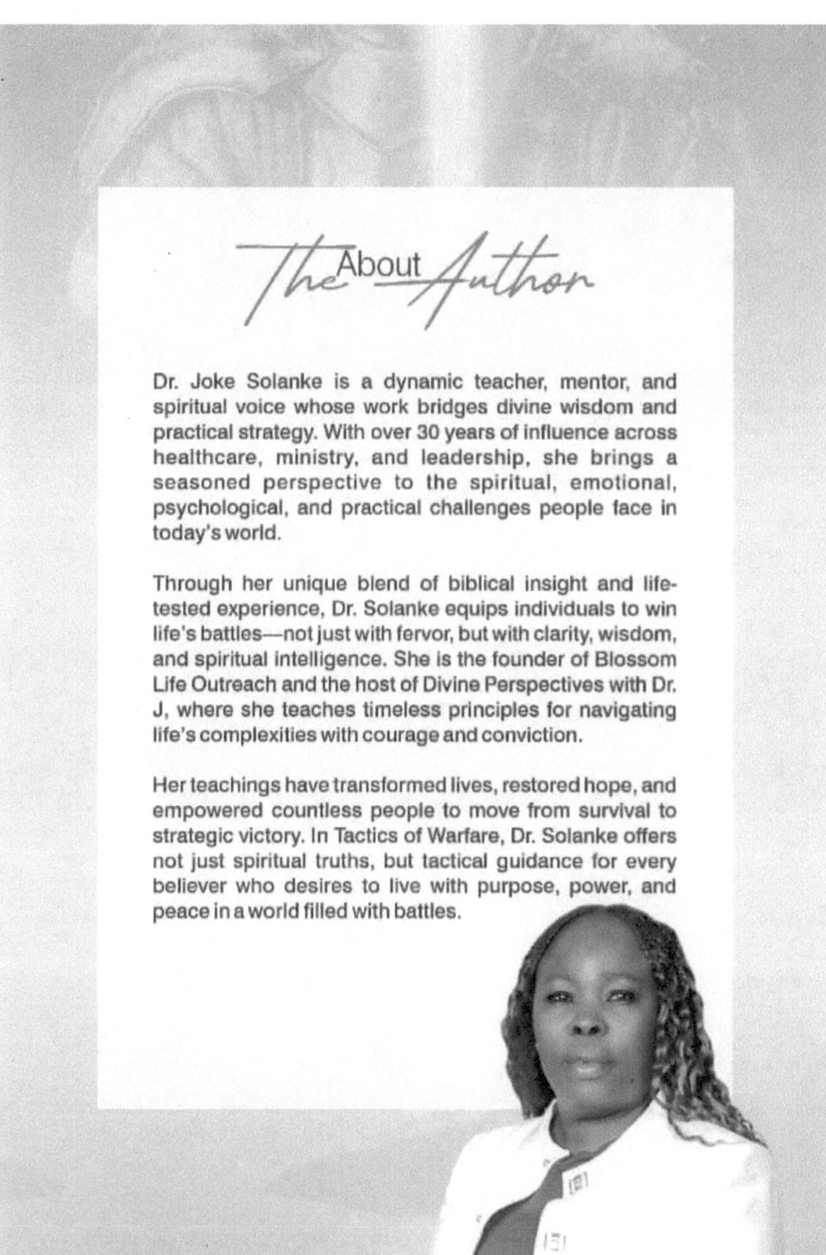

The About Author

Dr. Joke Solanke is a dynamic teacher, mentor, and spiritual voice whose work bridges divine wisdom and practical strategy. With over 30 years of influence across healthcare, ministry, and leadership, she brings a seasoned perspective to the spiritual, emotional, psychological, and practical challenges people face in today's world.

Through her unique blend of biblical insight and life-tested experience, Dr. Solanke equips individuals to win life's battles—not just with fervor, but with clarity, wisdom, and spiritual intelligence. She is the founder of Blossom Life Outreach and the host of Divine Perspectives with Dr. J, where she teaches timeless principles for navigating life's complexities with courage and conviction.

Her teachings have transformed lives, restored hope, and empowered countless people to move from survival to strategic victory. In Tactics of Warfare, Dr. Solanke offers not just spiritual truths, but tactical guidance for every believer who desires to live with purpose, power, and peace in a world filled with battles.

www.ingramcontent.com/pod-product-compliance
Lightning Source LLC
LaVergne TN
LVHW041055080826
845145LV00007B/1582

* 9 7 8 1 9 6 8 7 1 7 1 5 5 *